COLORING MANDALAS FOR ADULTS AND CHILDREN

The Ultimate Antistress Book

Lumina Visions

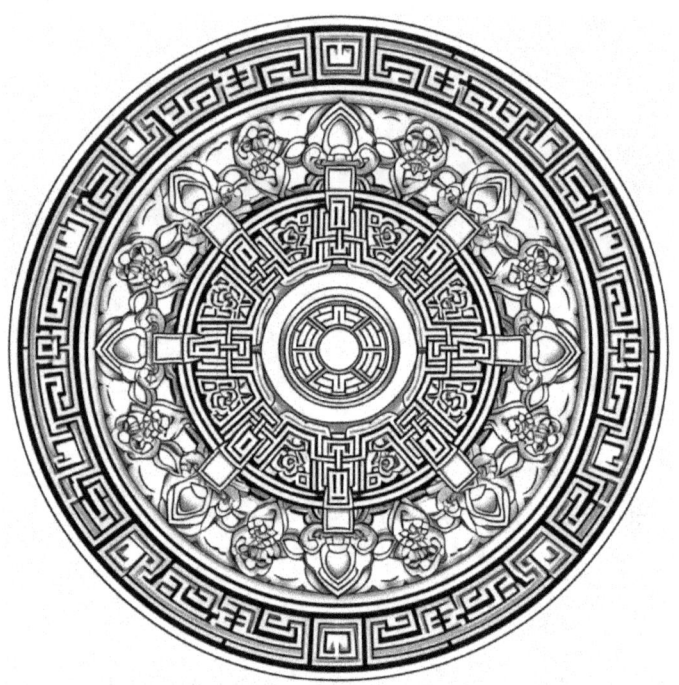

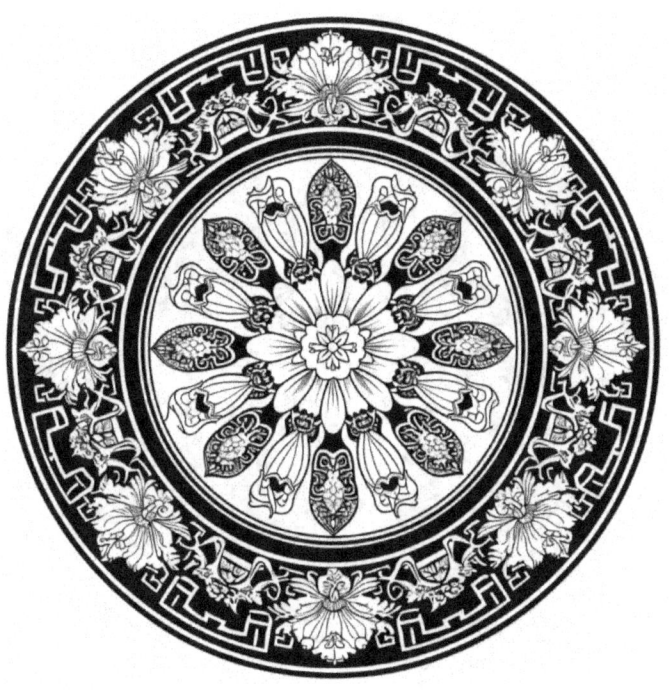

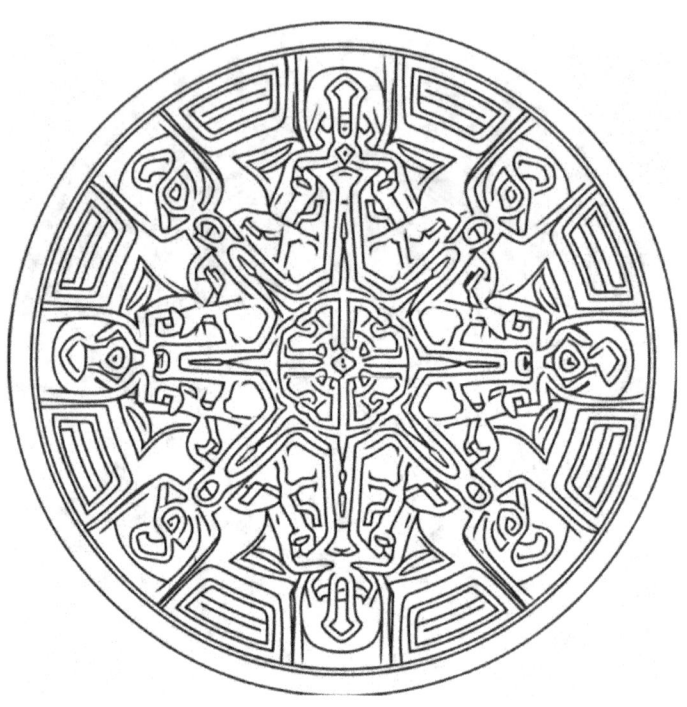

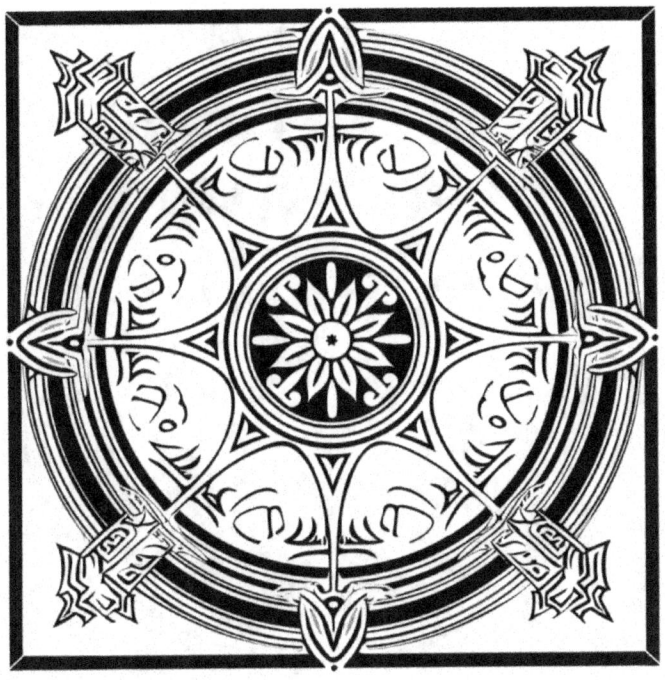

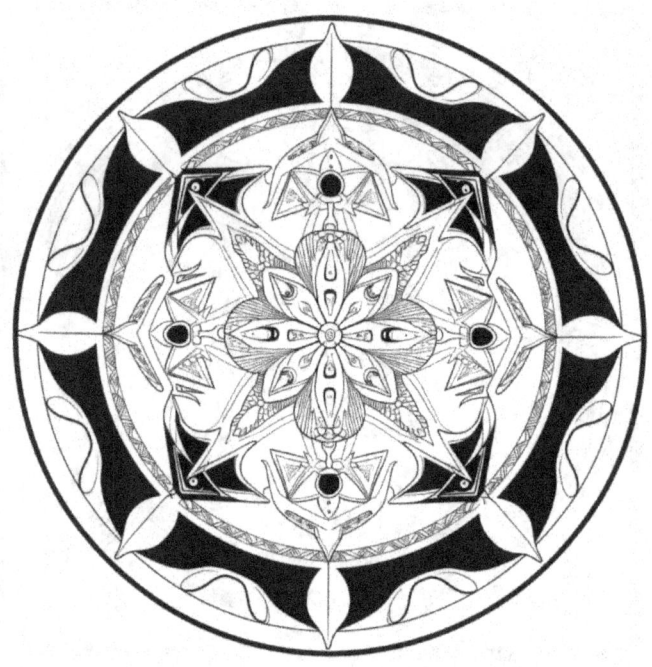

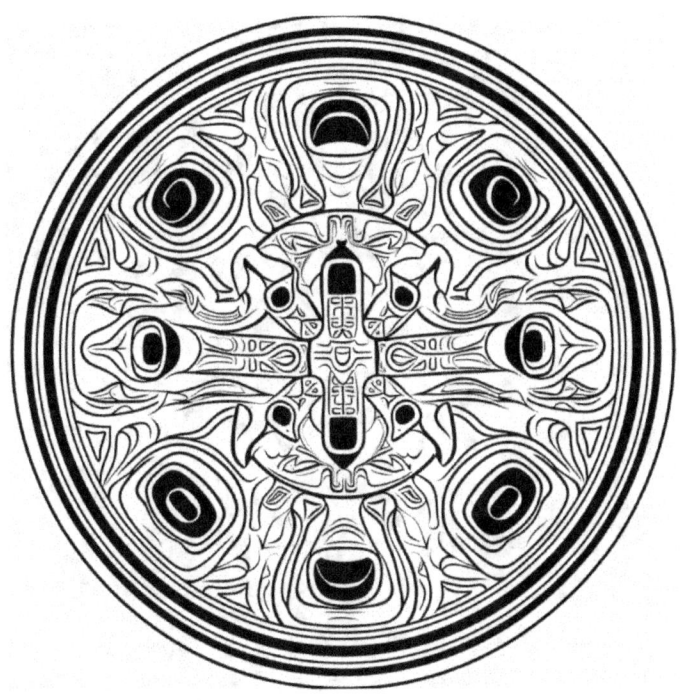

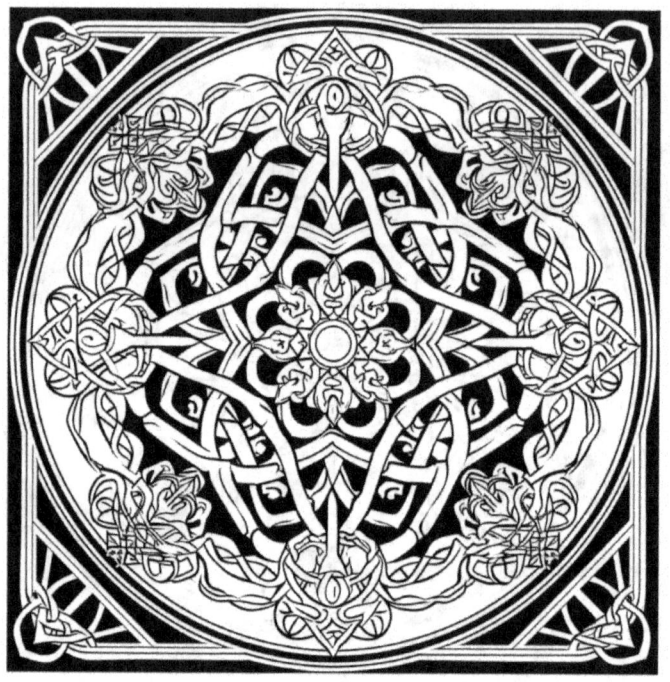

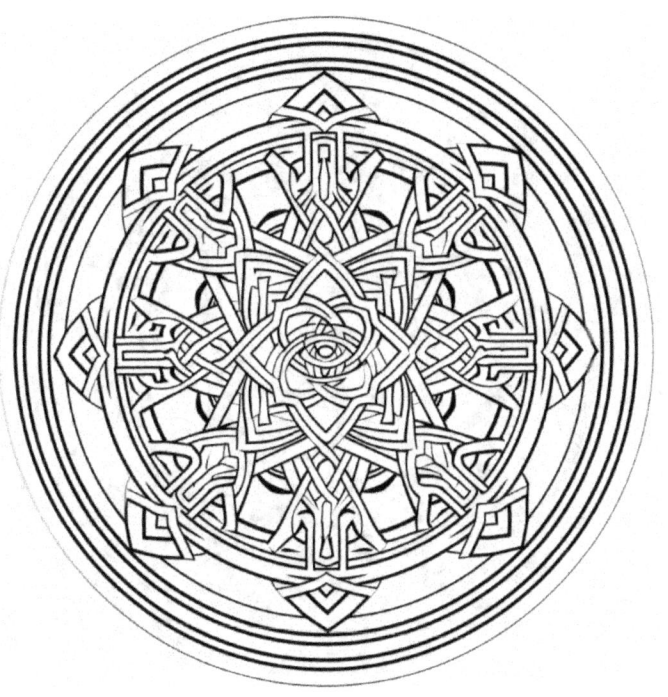

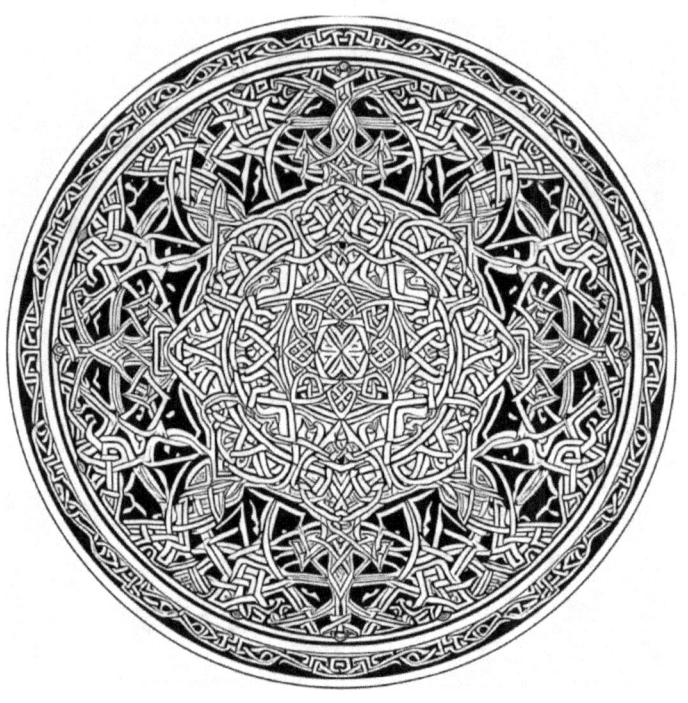

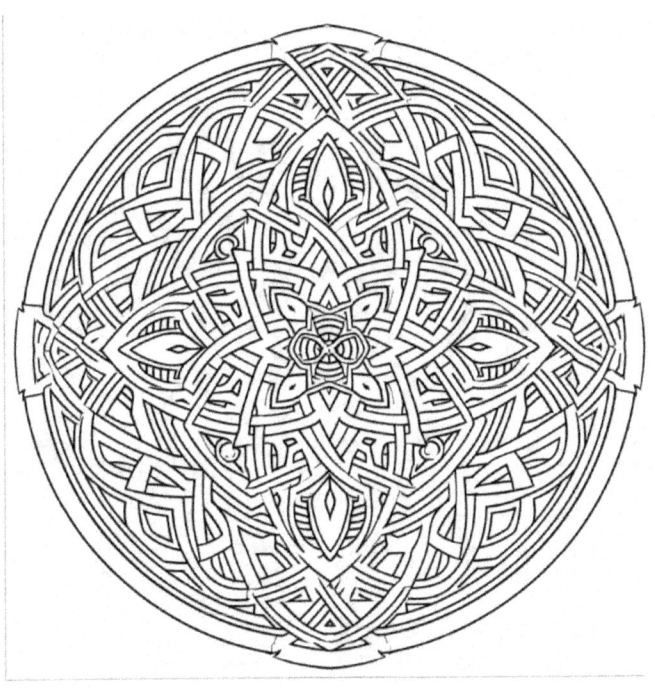

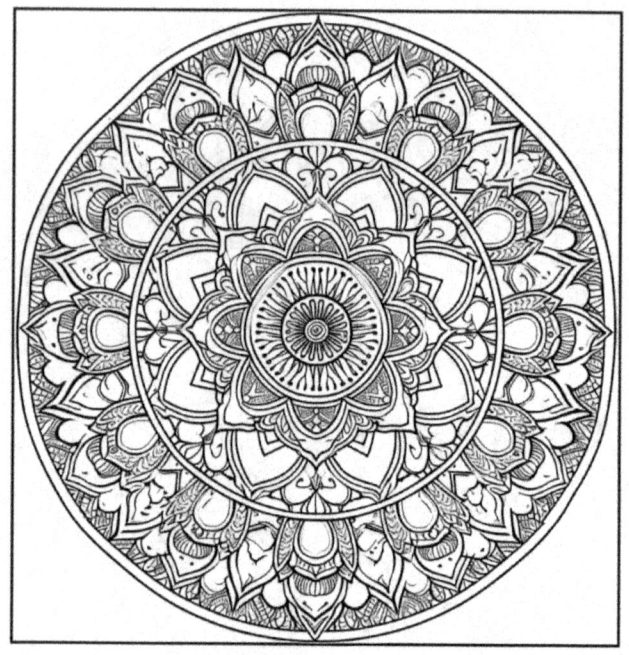

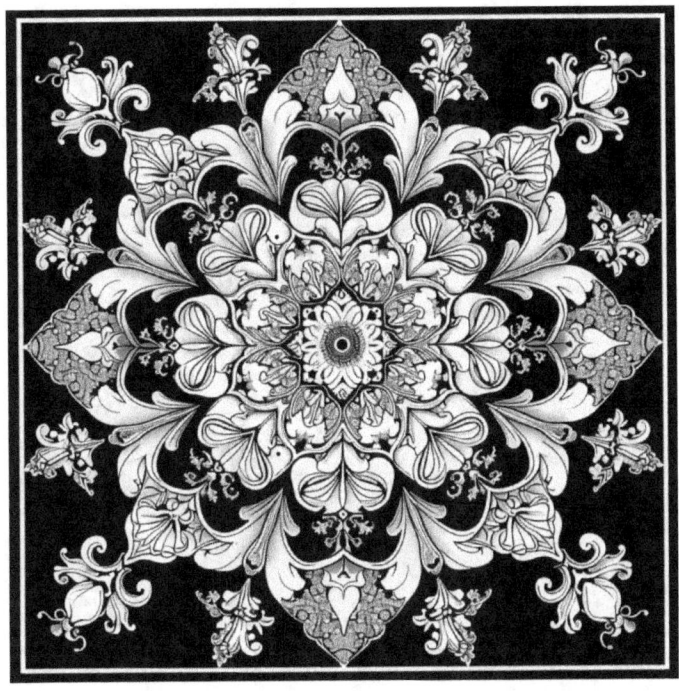

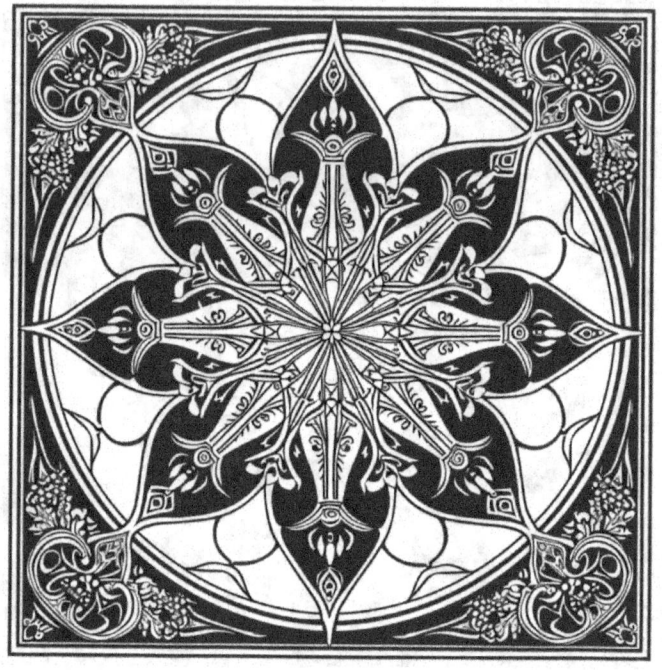

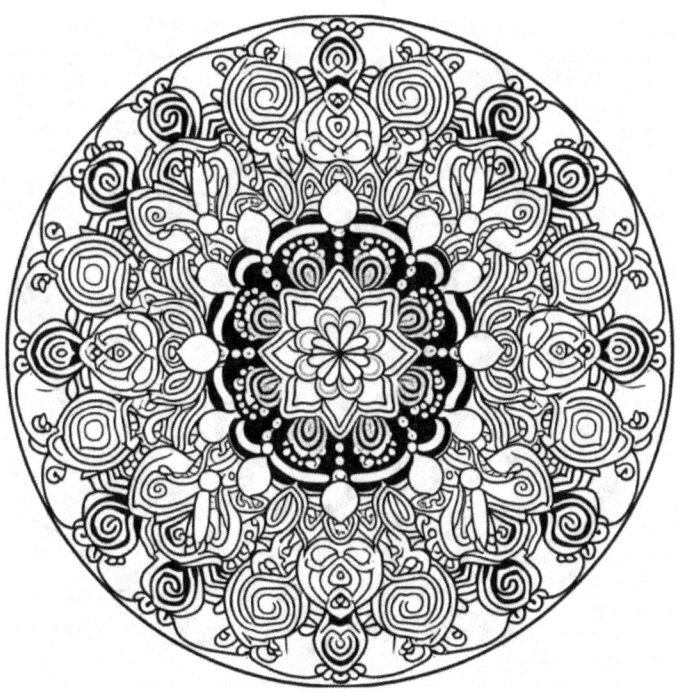

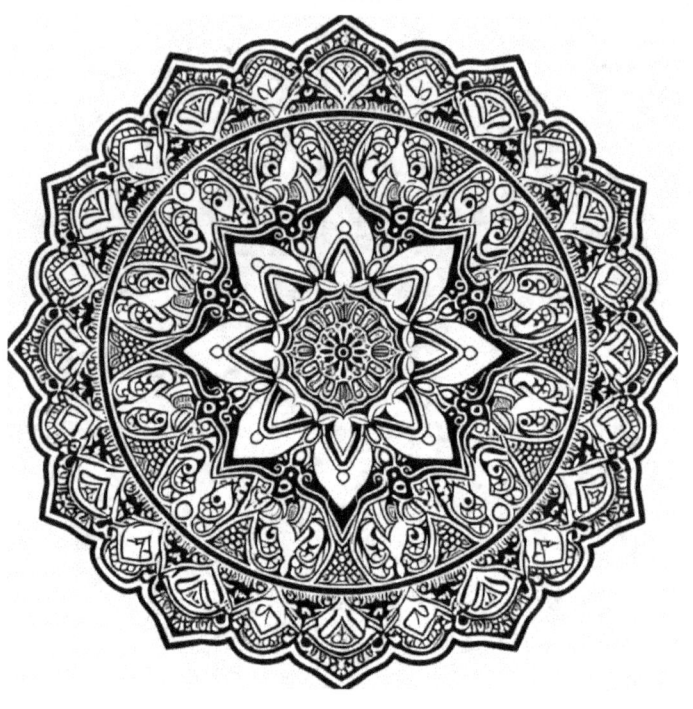

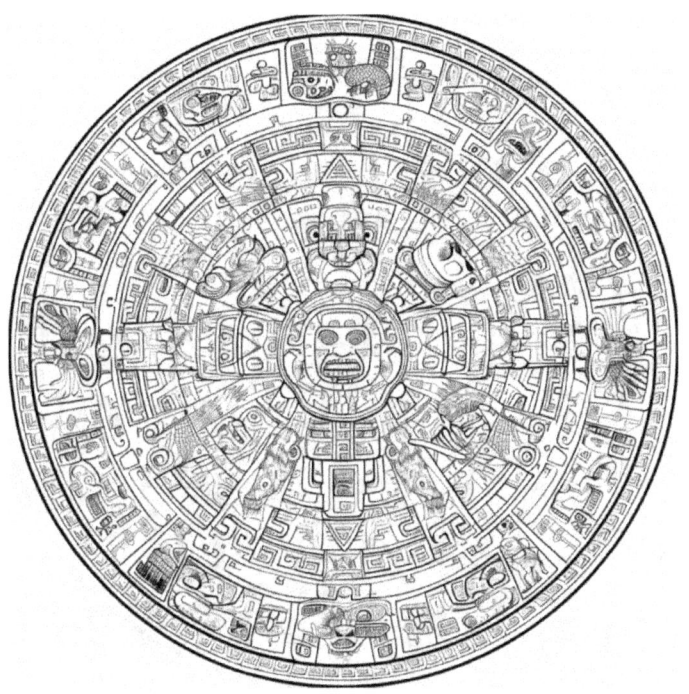

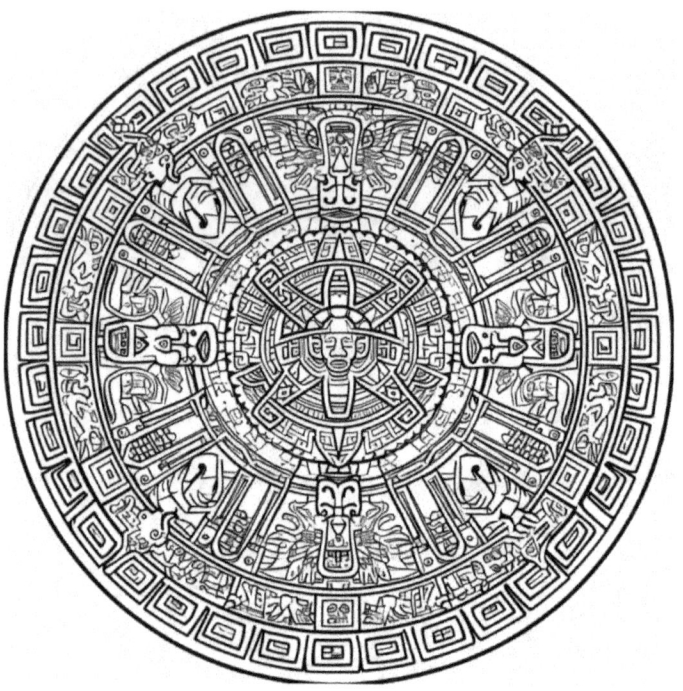

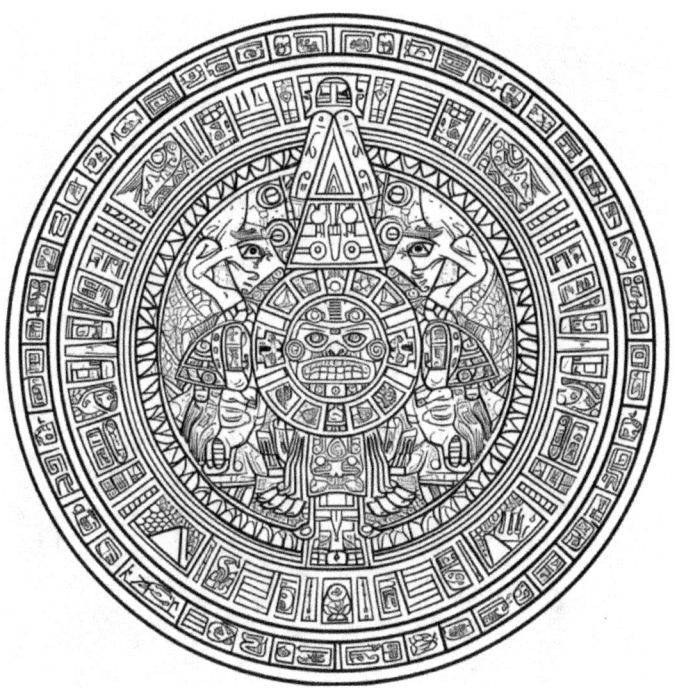

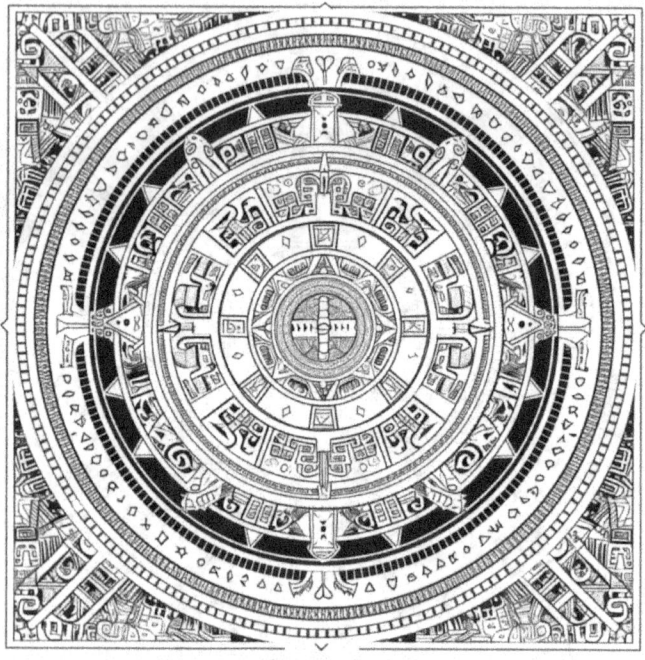

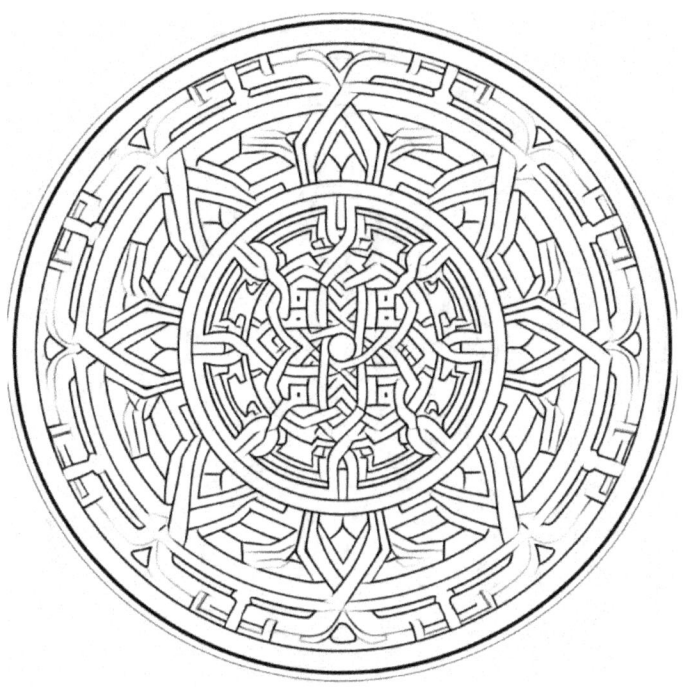

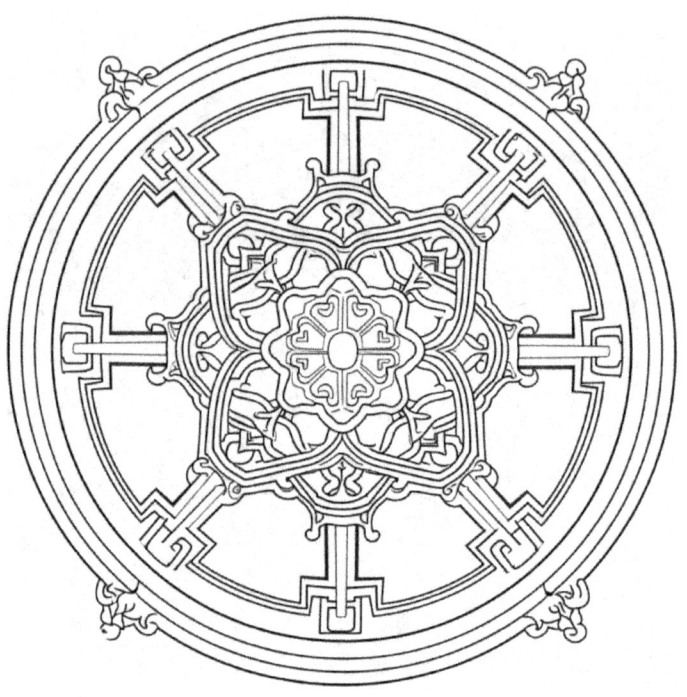

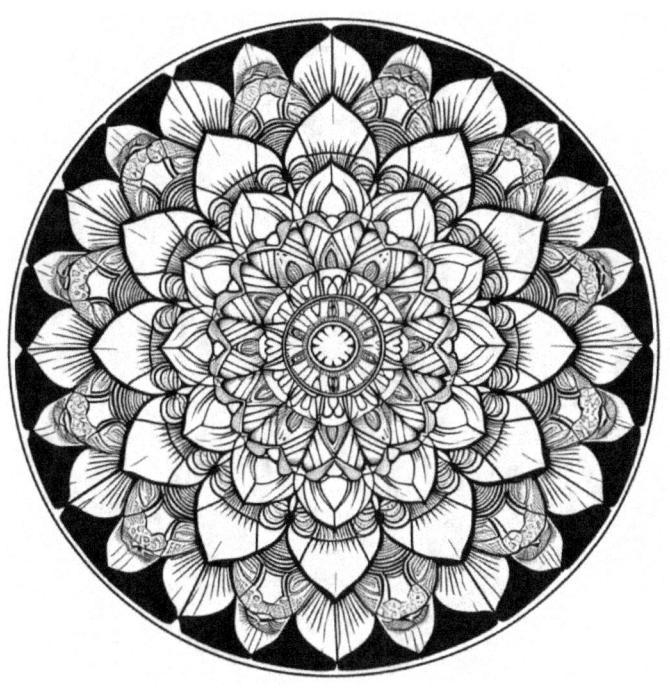

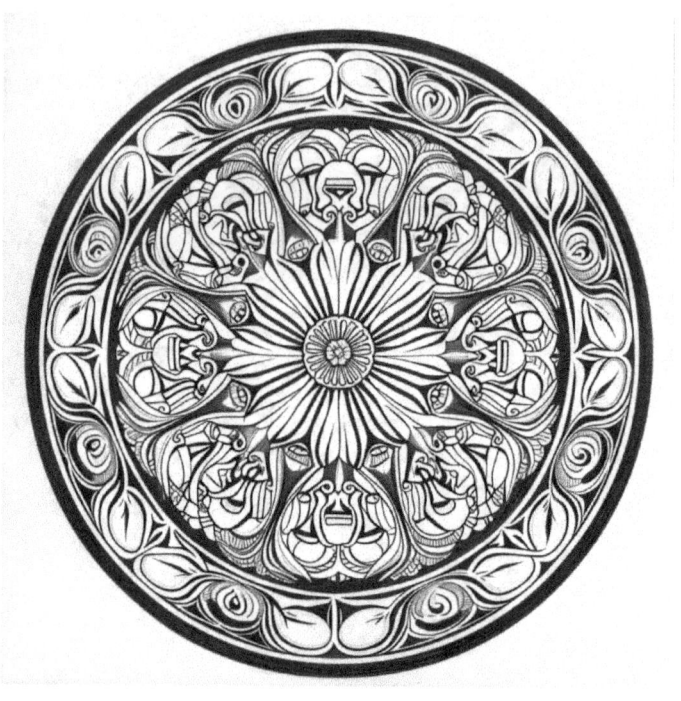

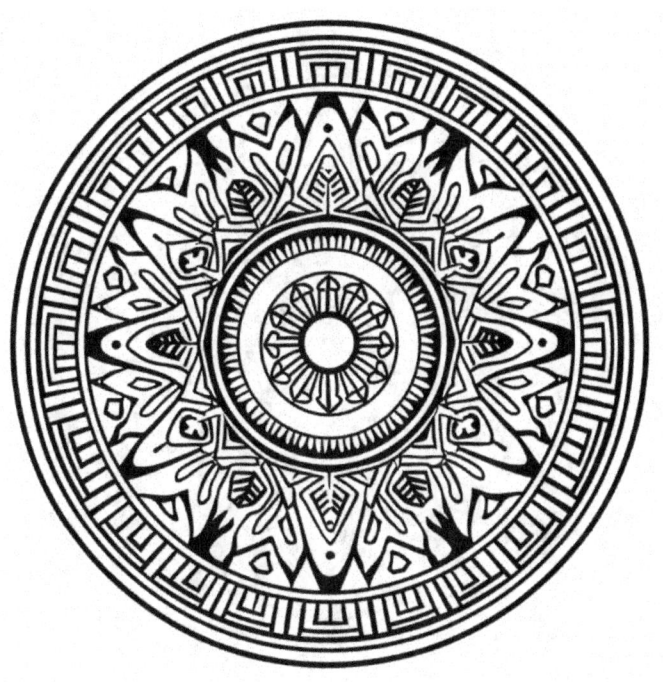

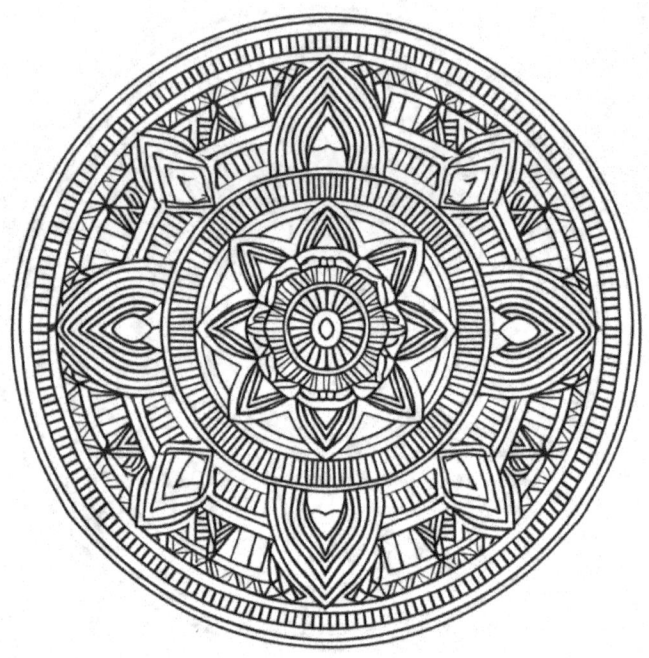

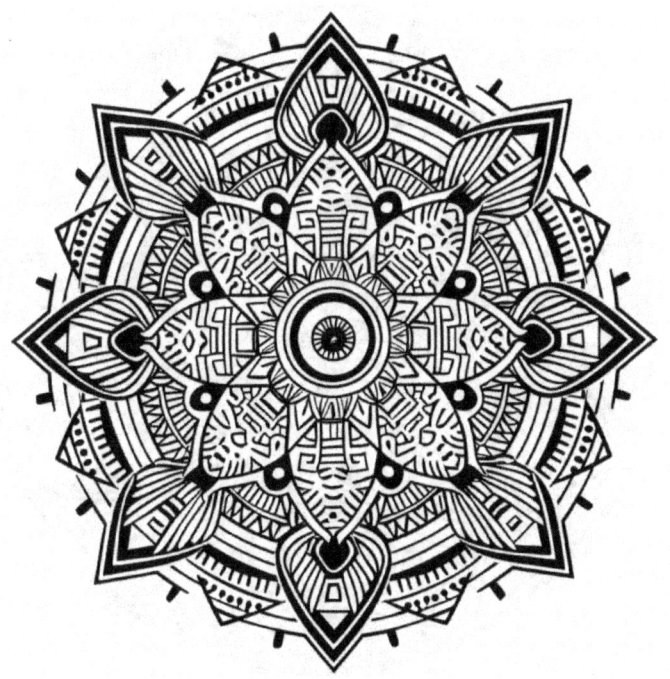

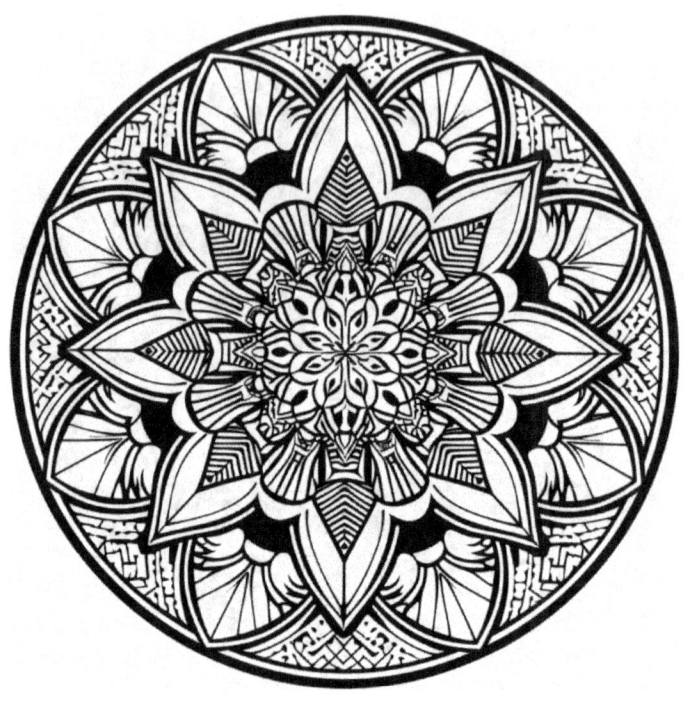

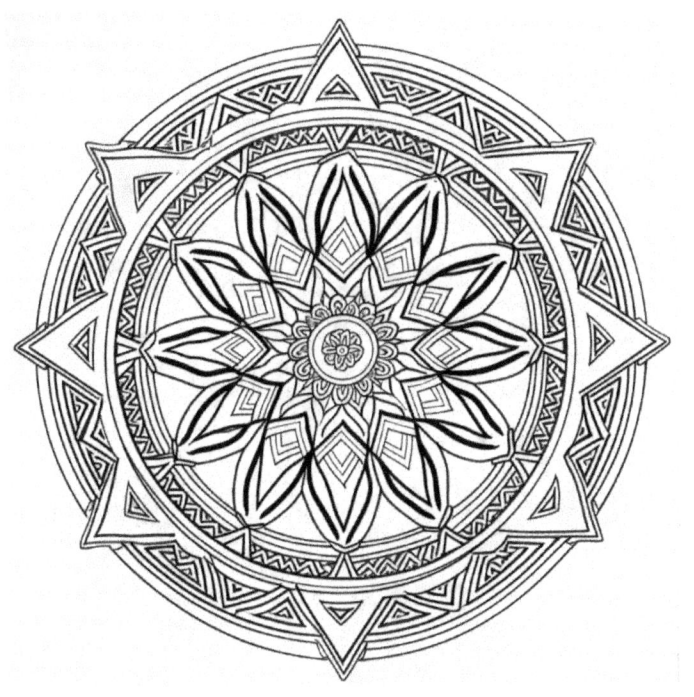

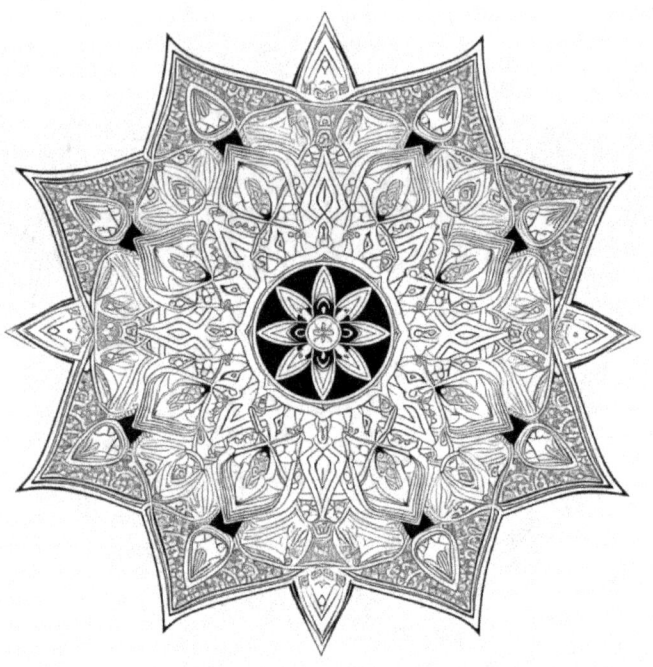

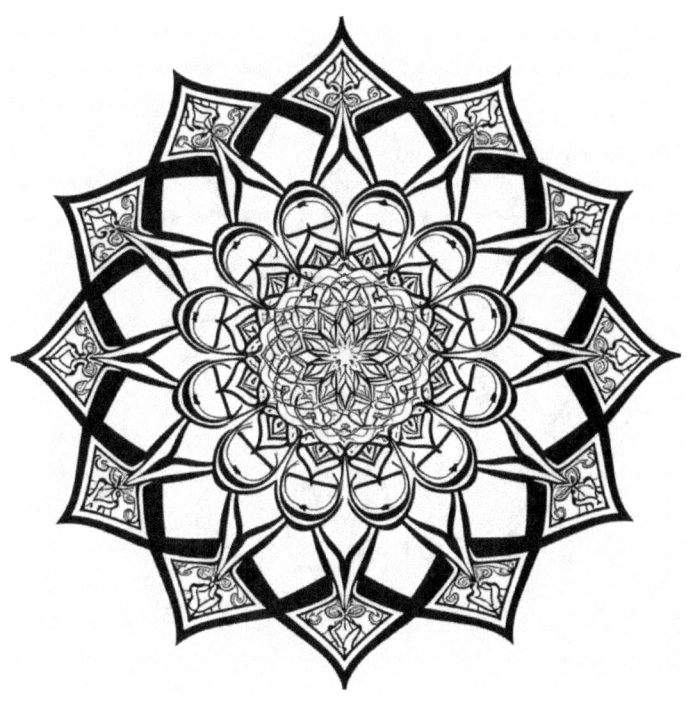

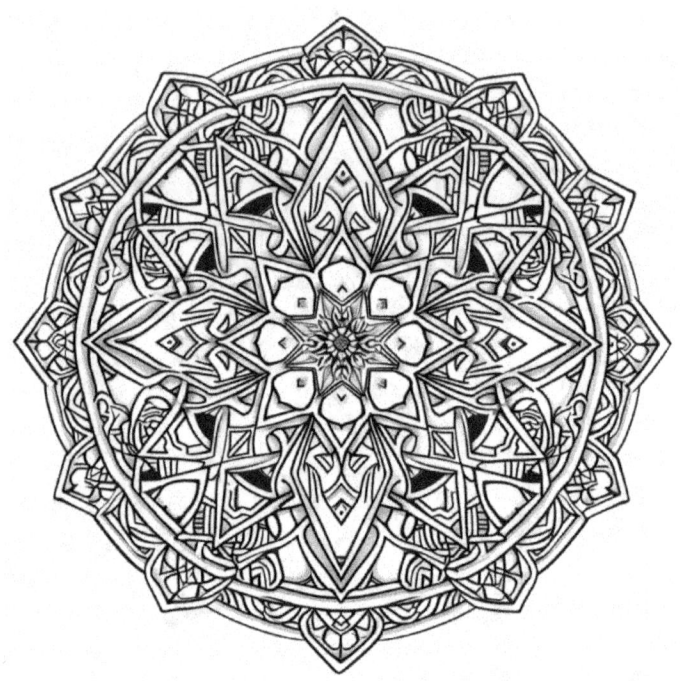

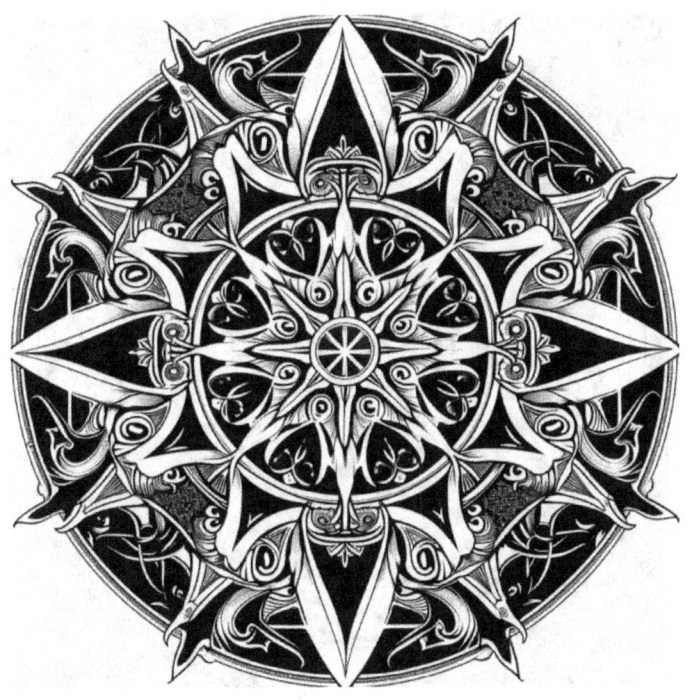

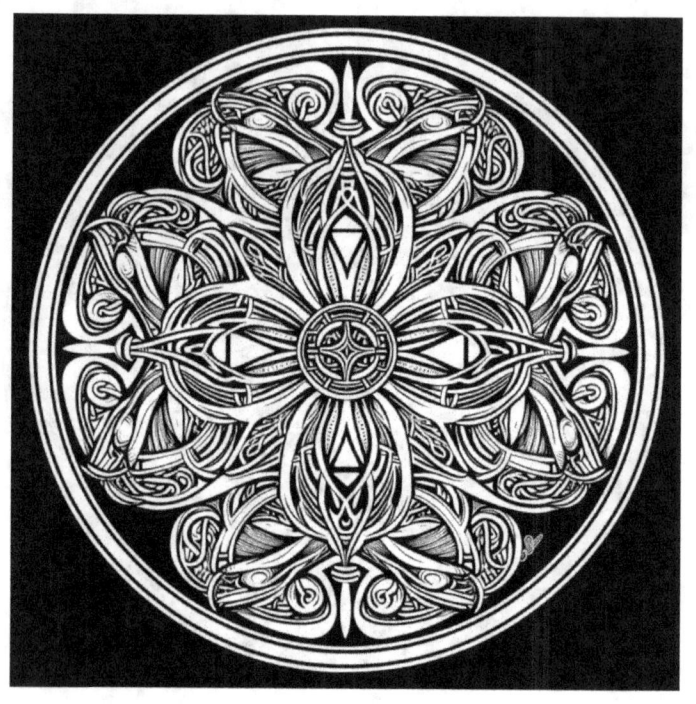

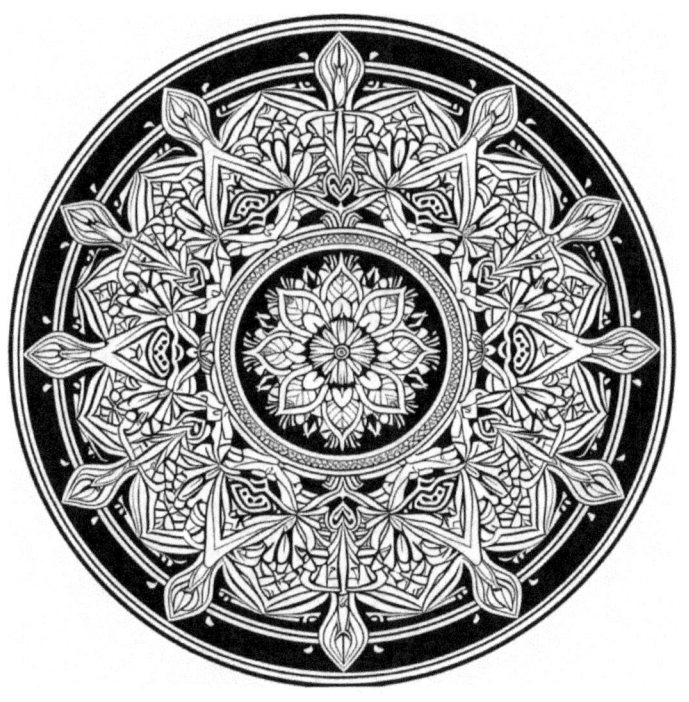

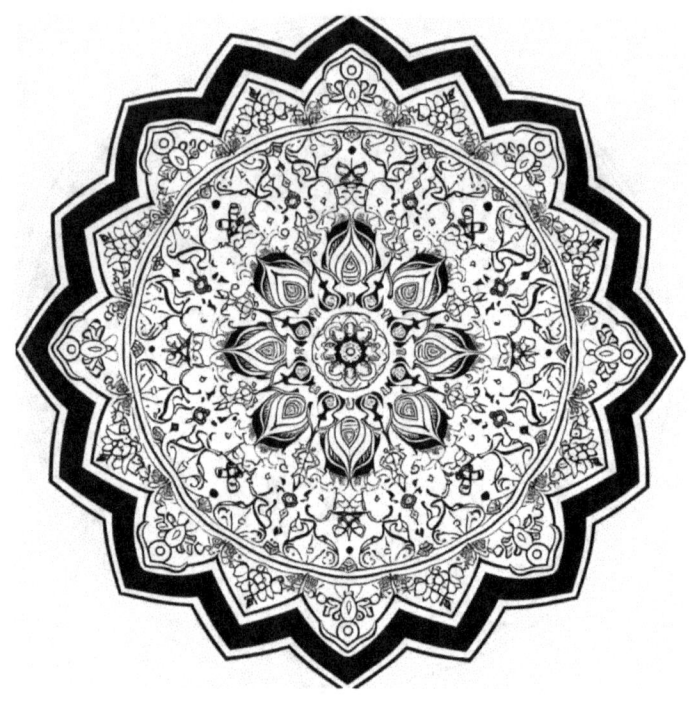

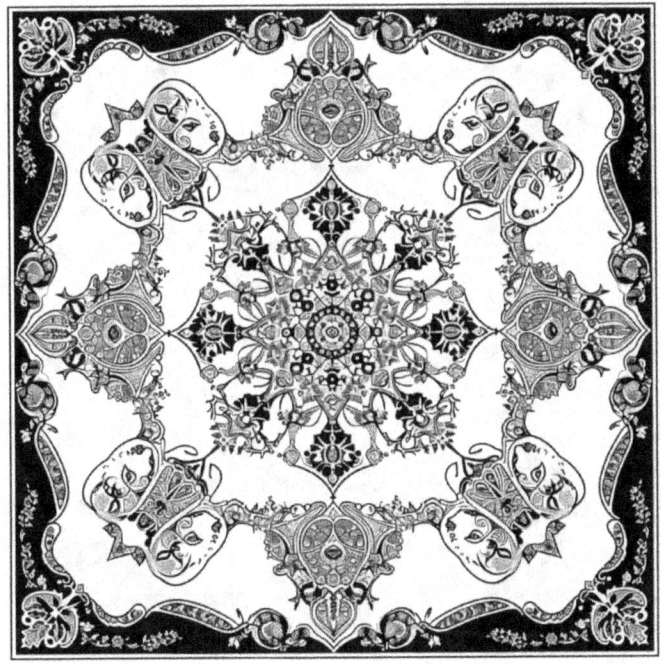

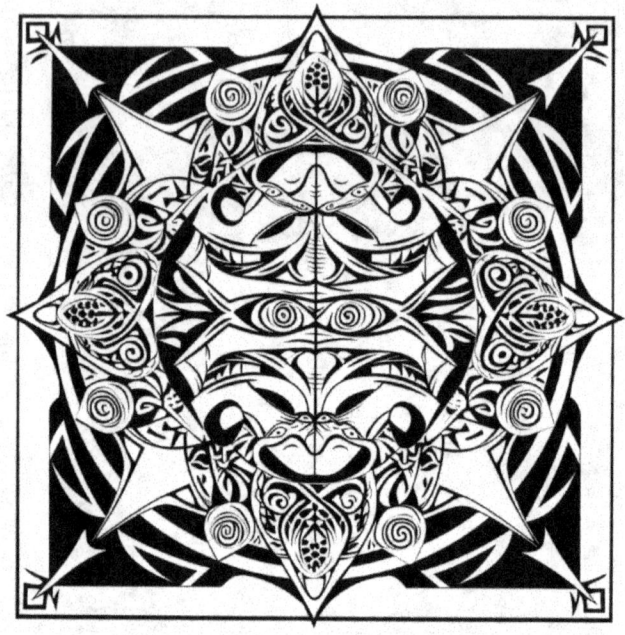

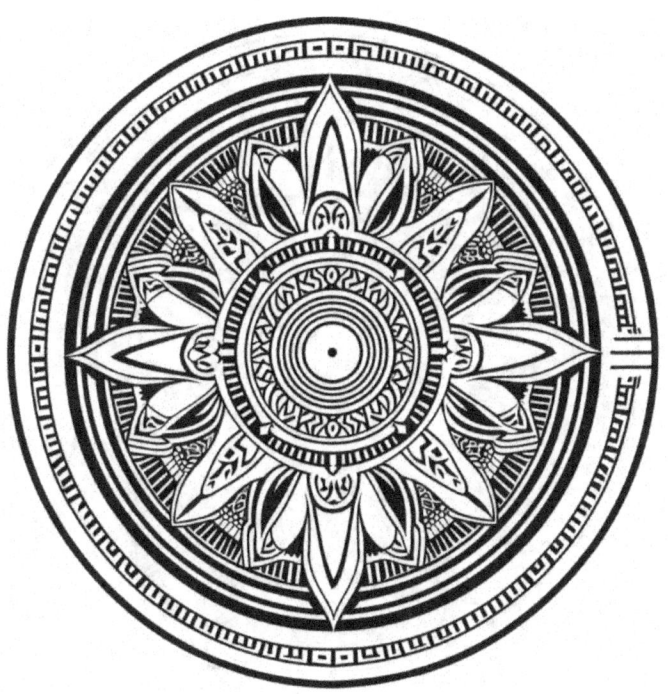

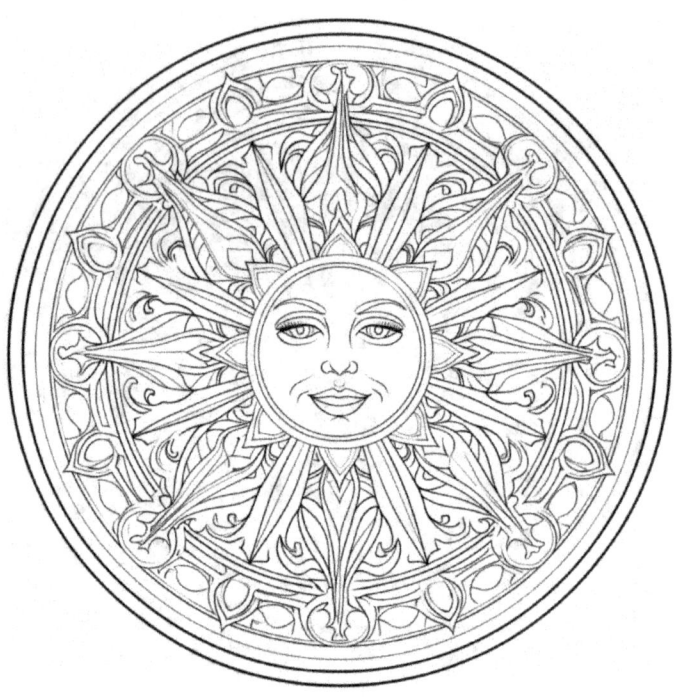

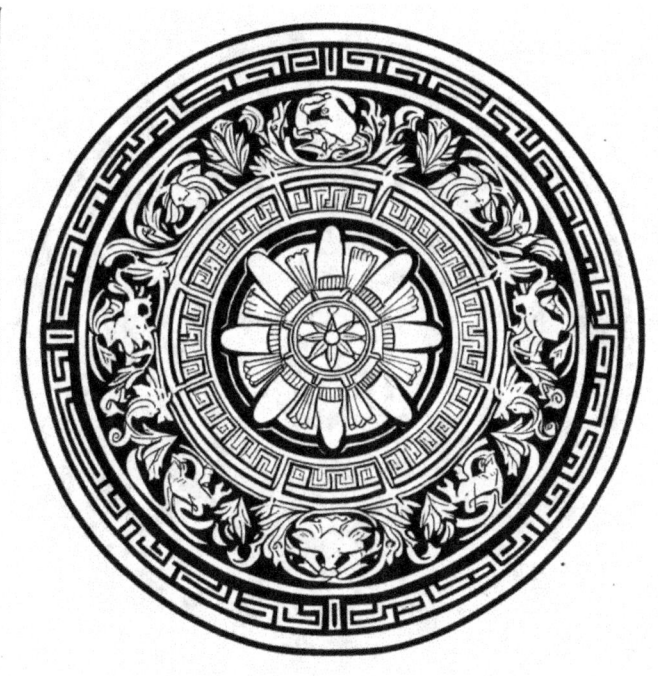

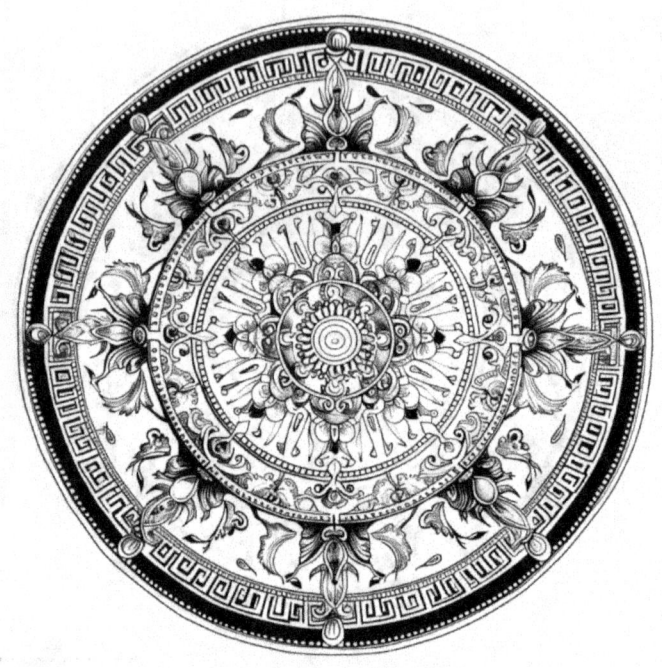

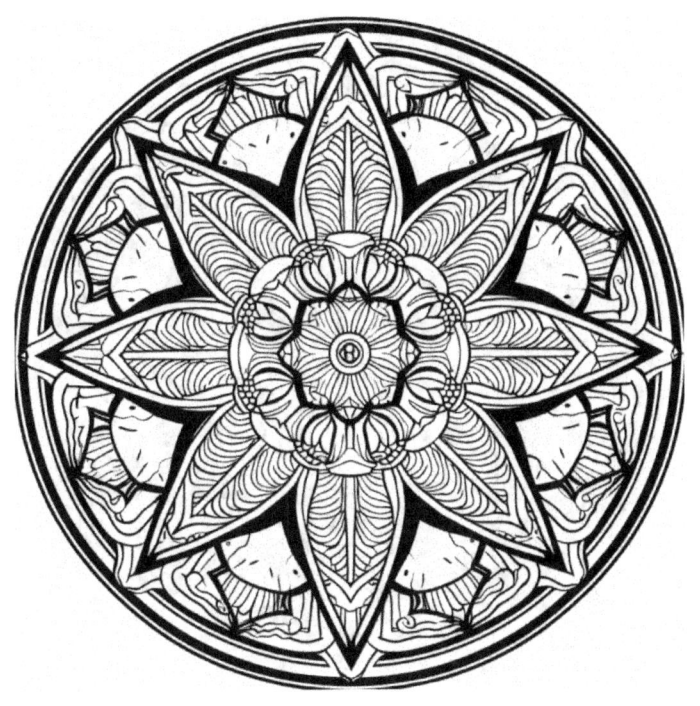

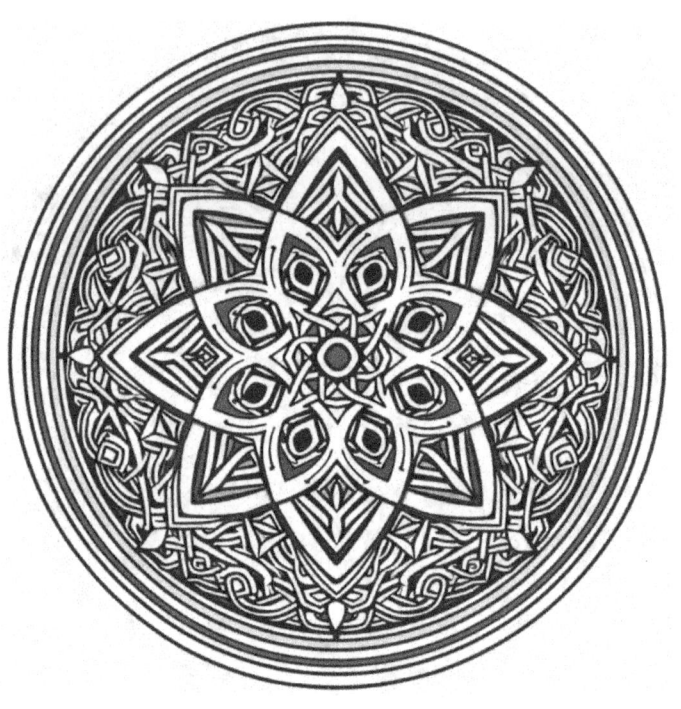

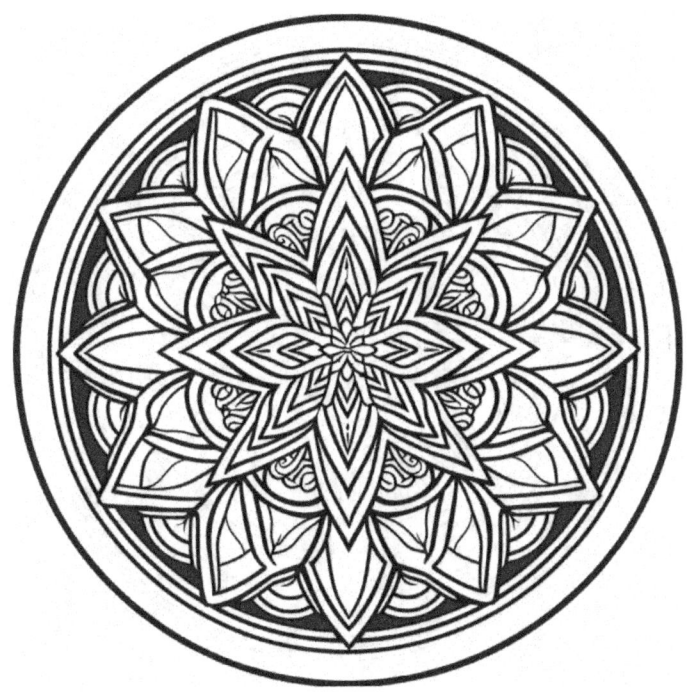

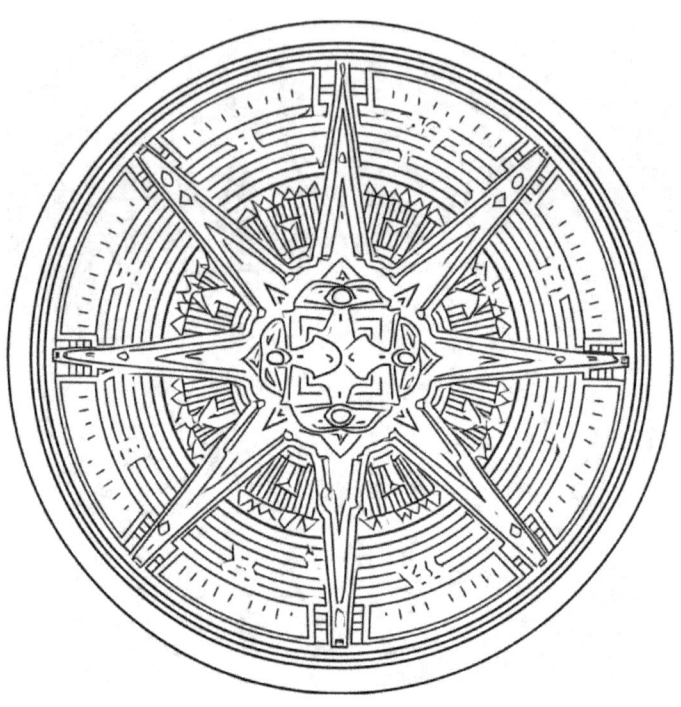

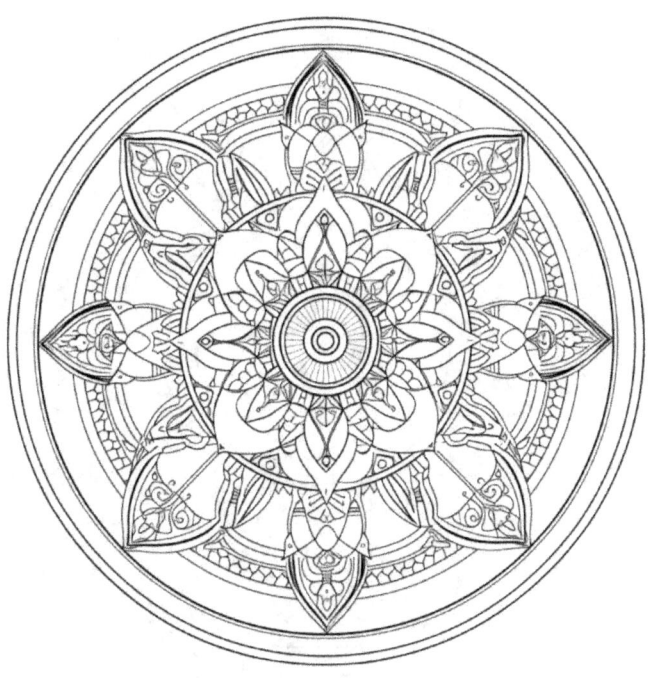

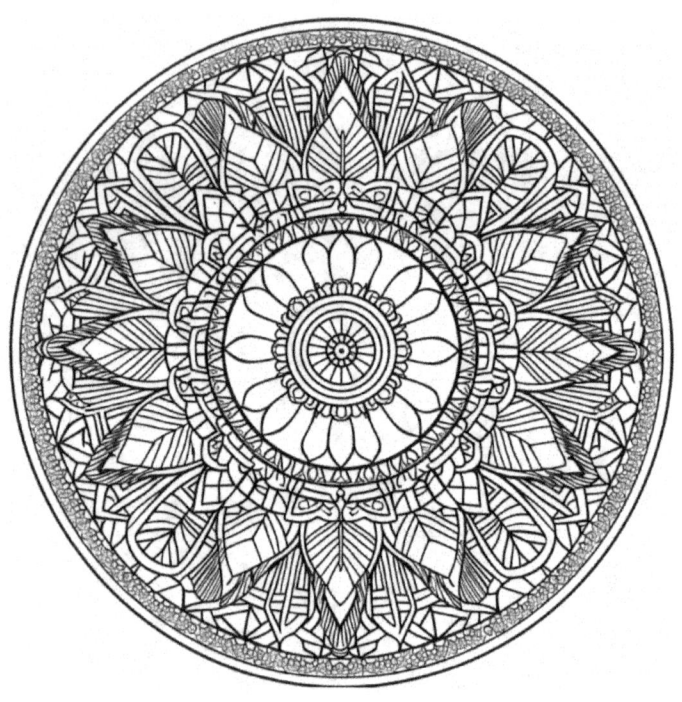

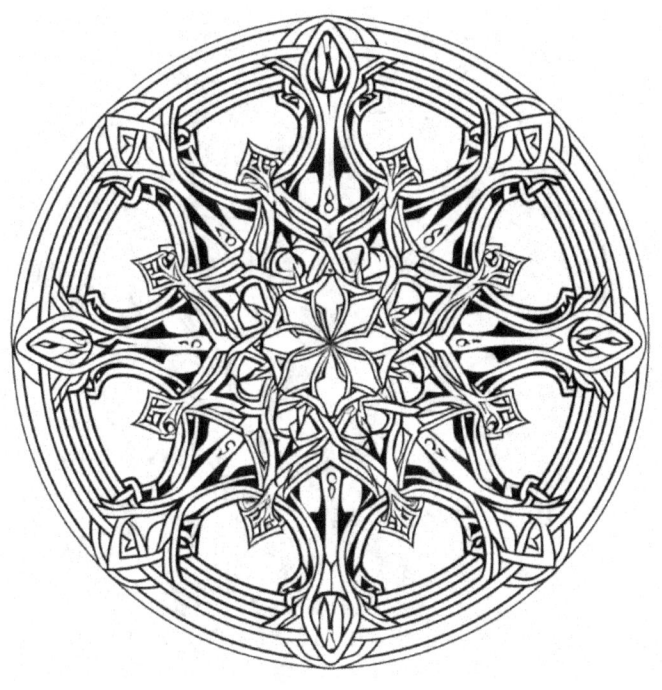

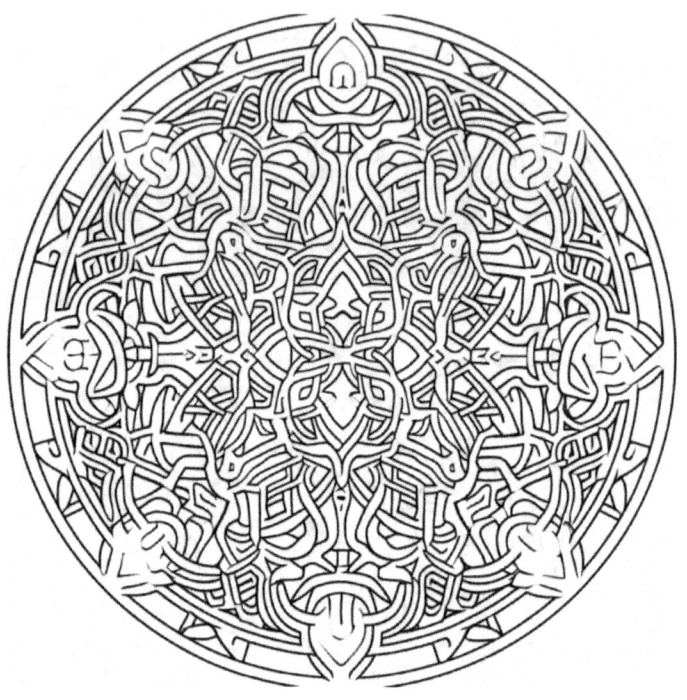

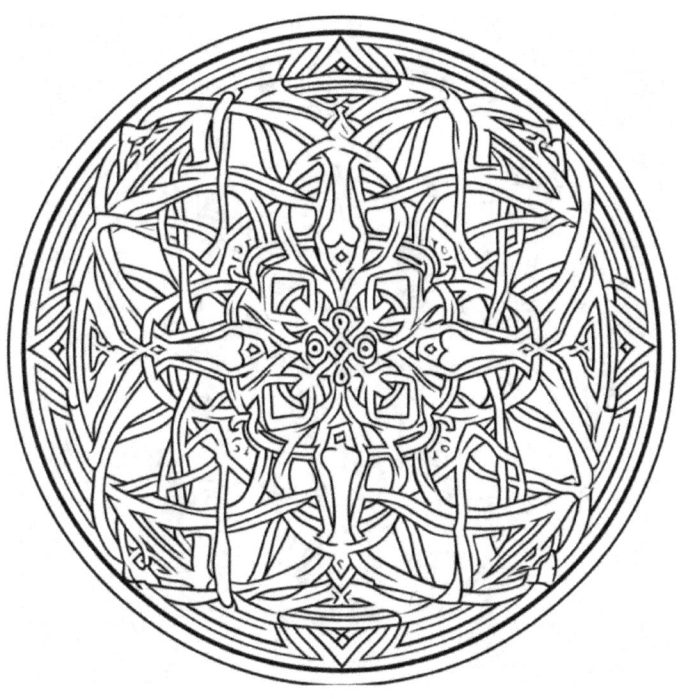

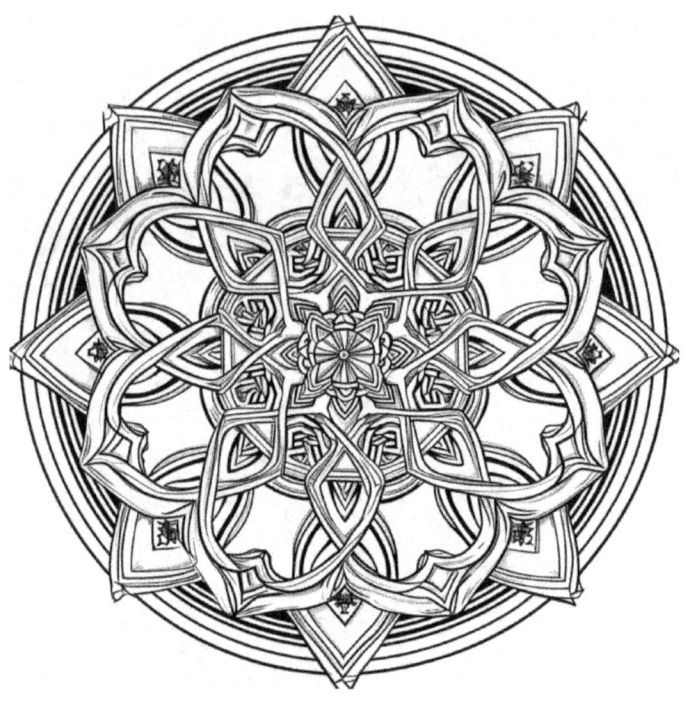

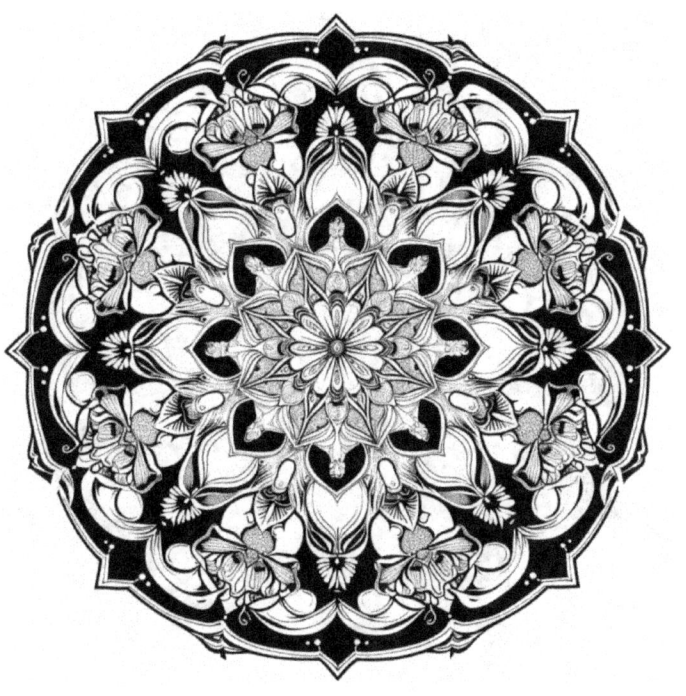

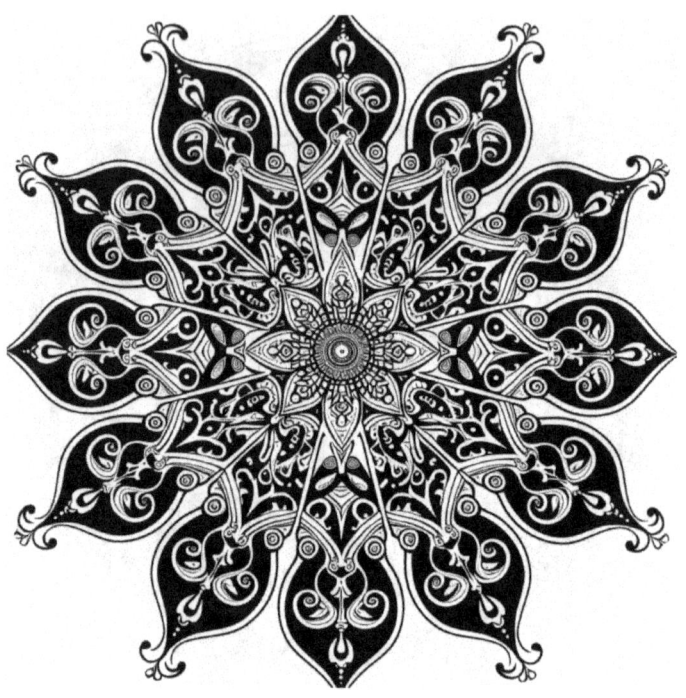

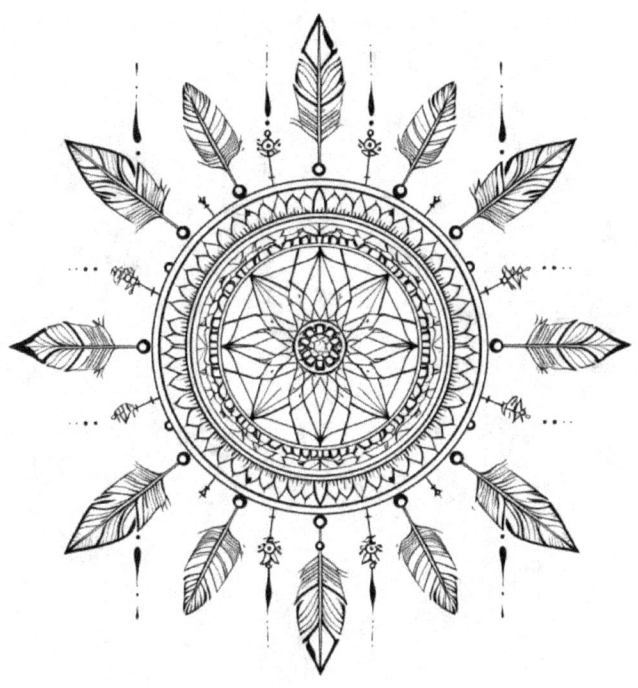

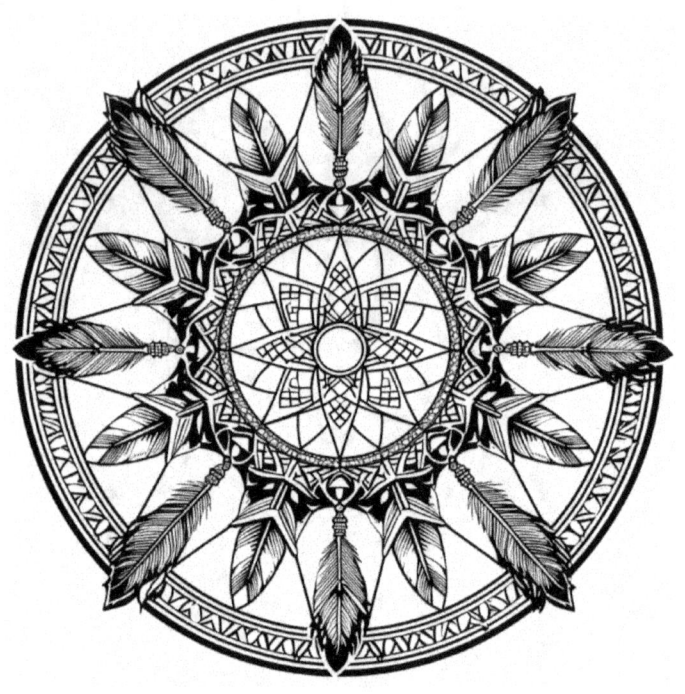

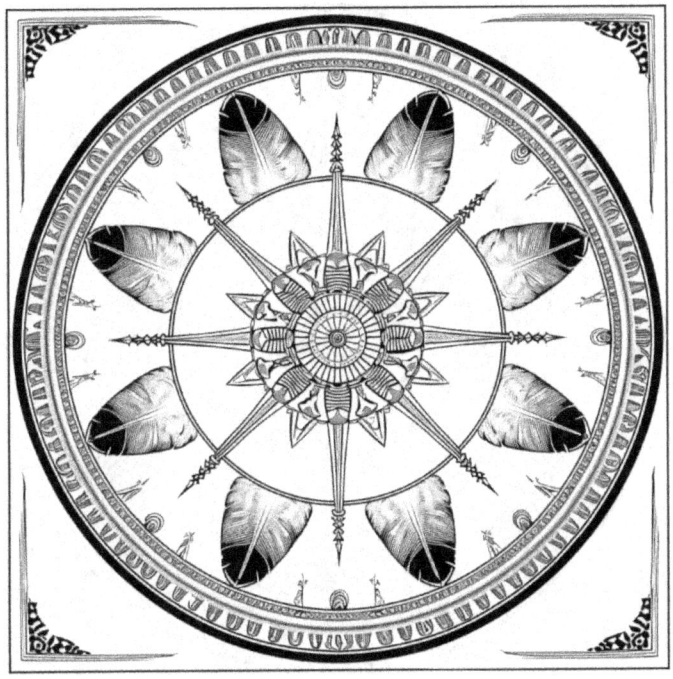

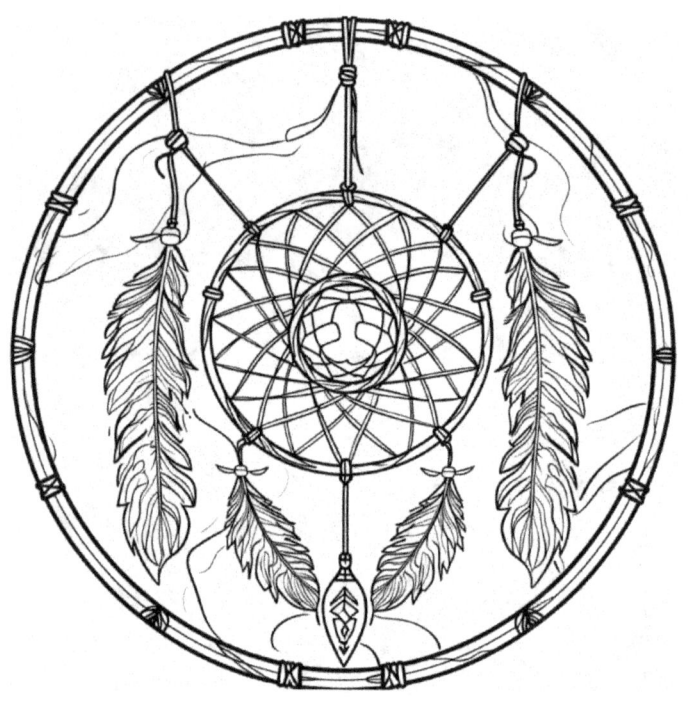

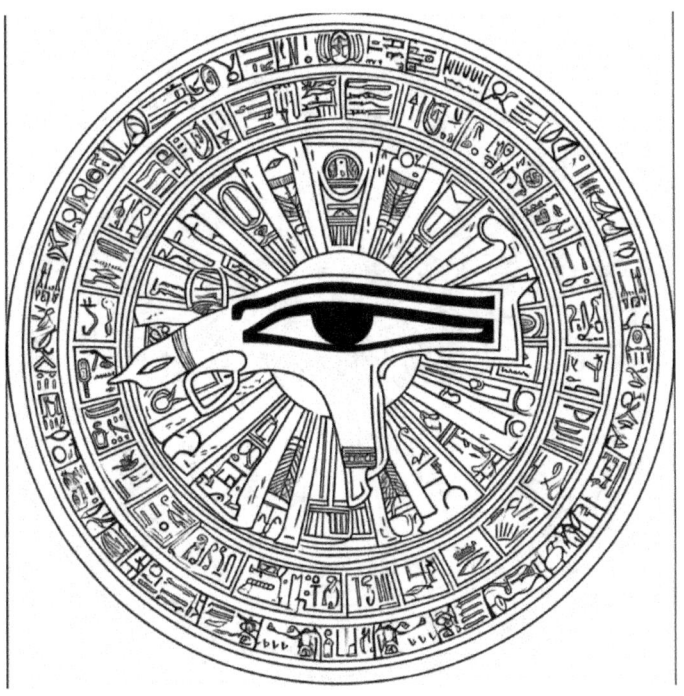

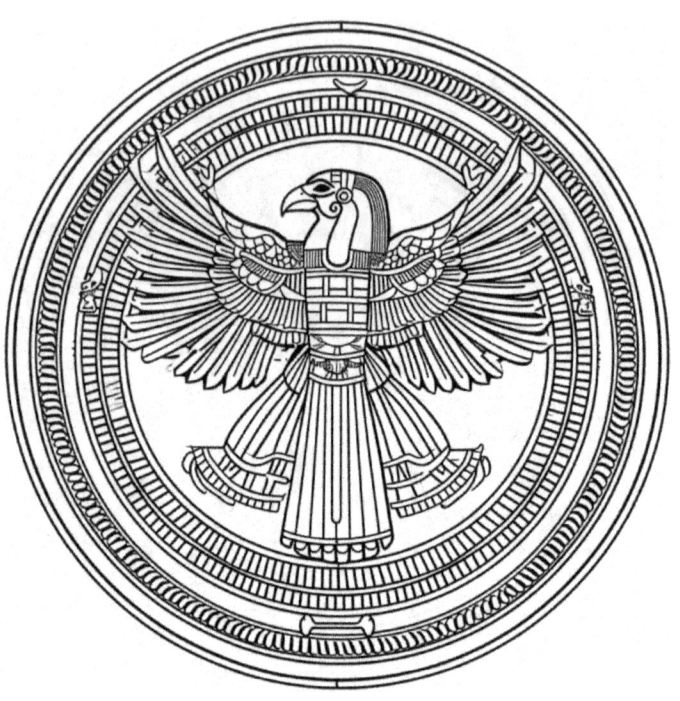

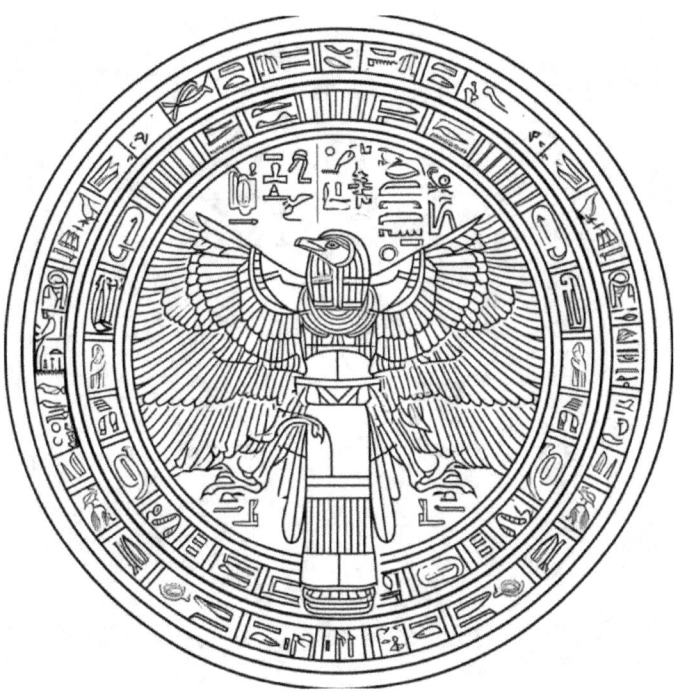

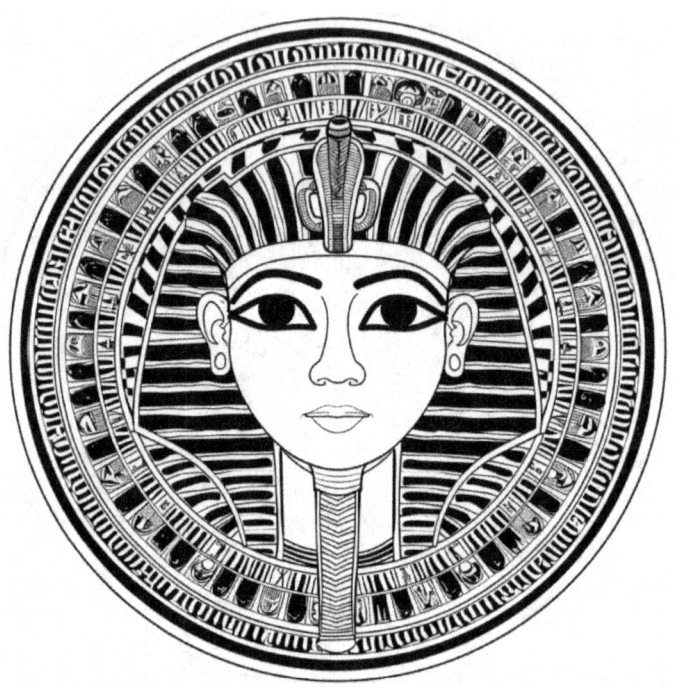

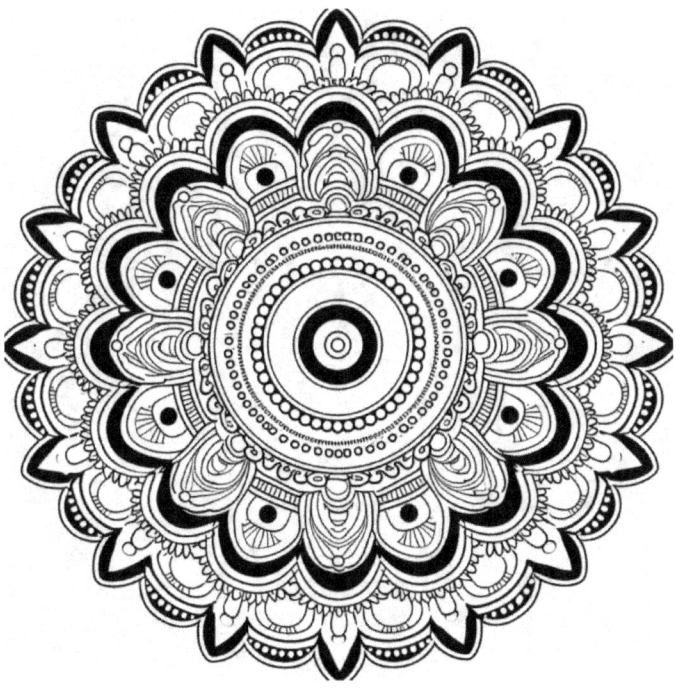

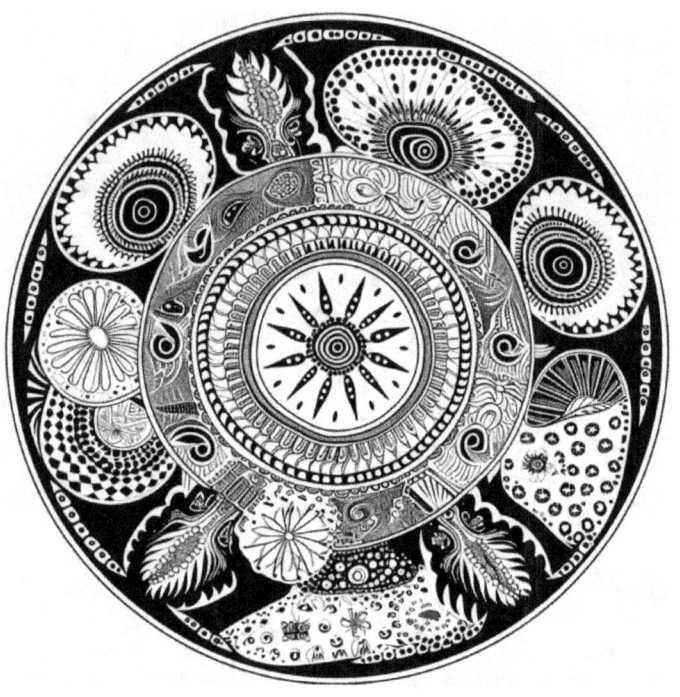

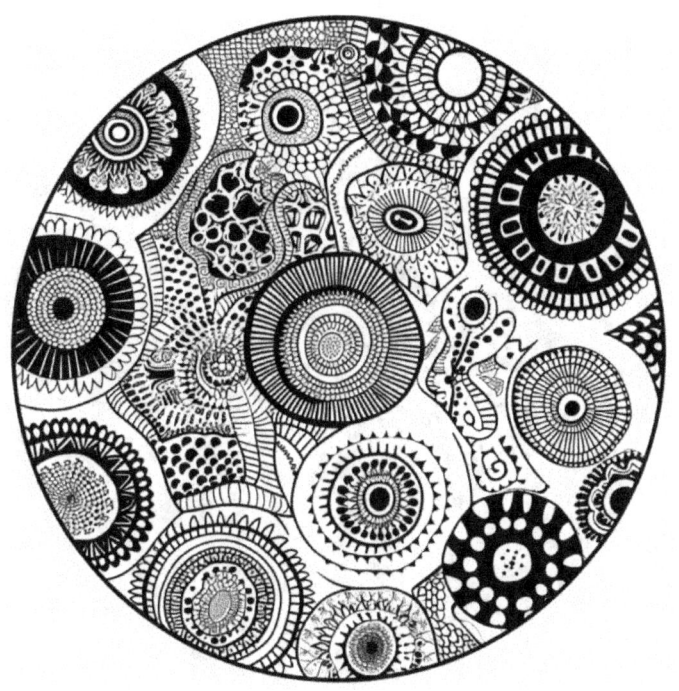

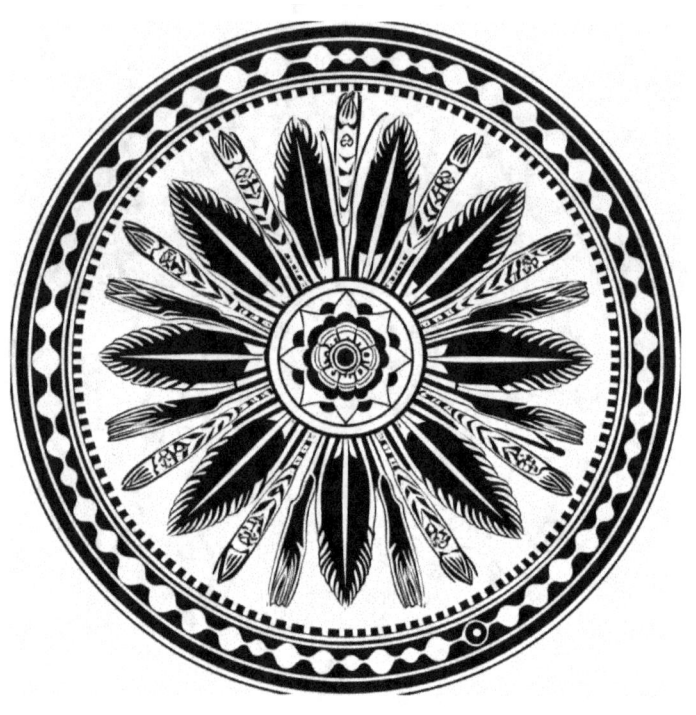

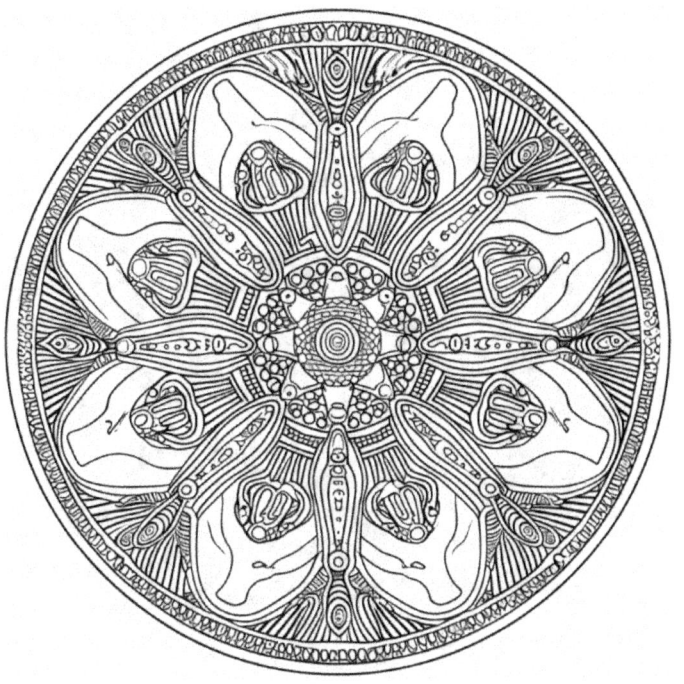

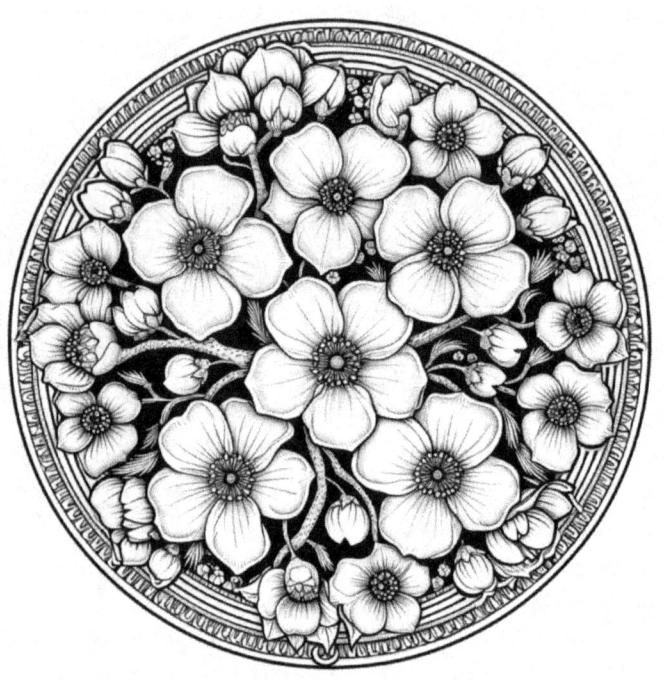

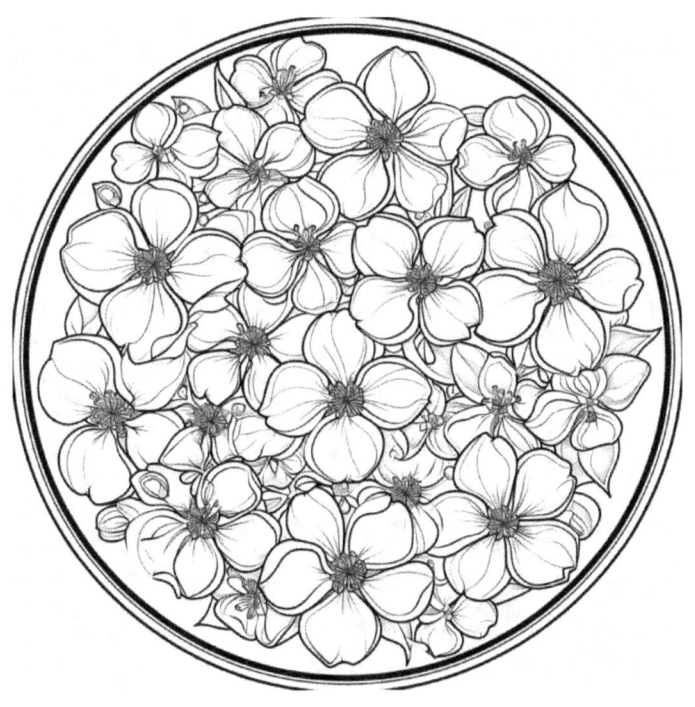

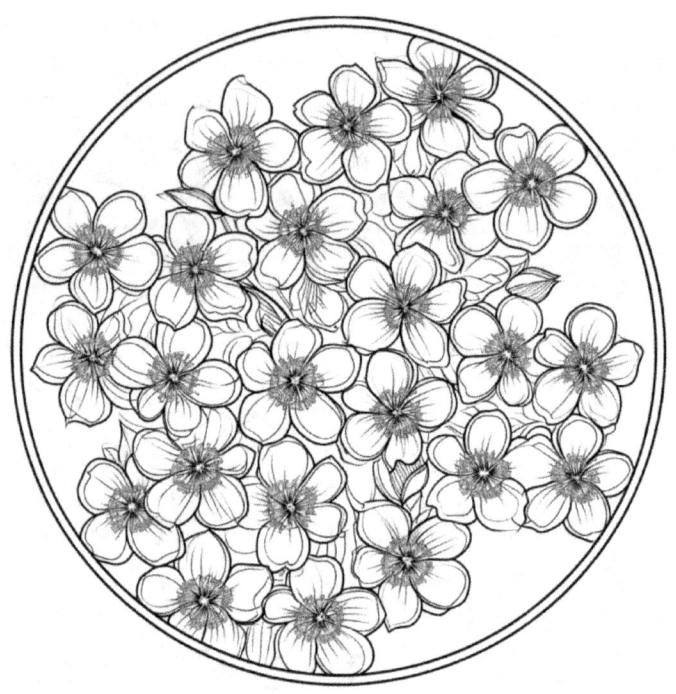

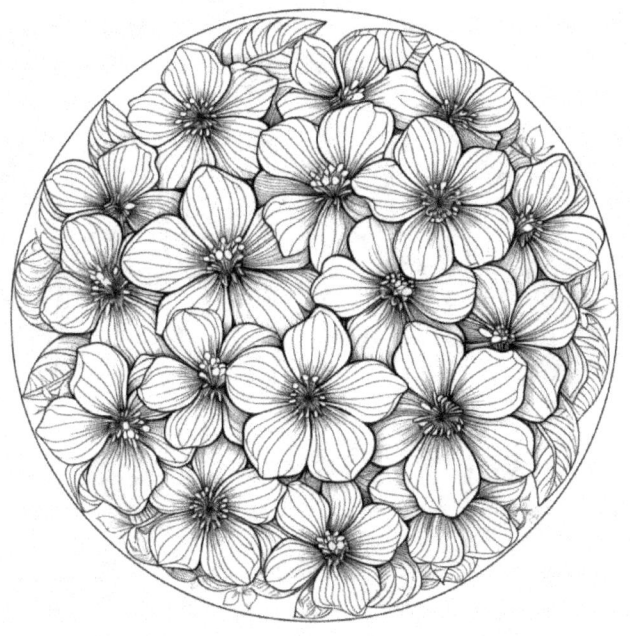

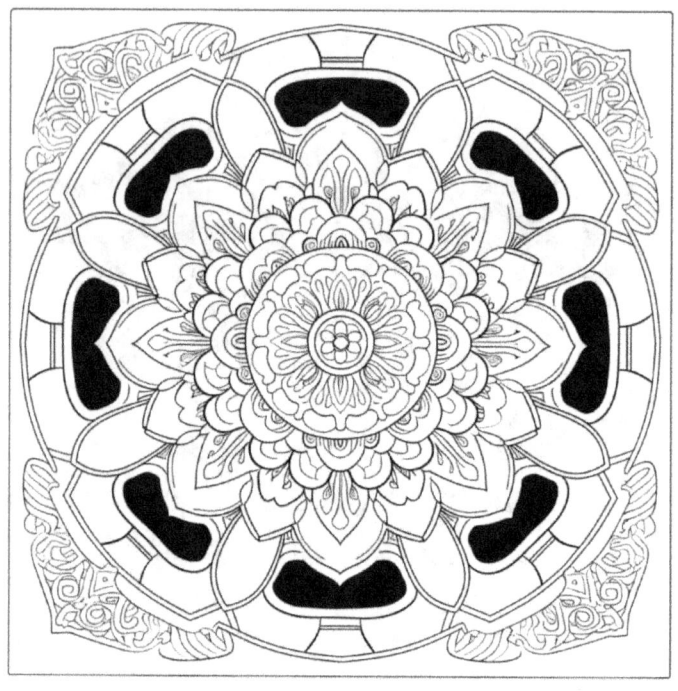

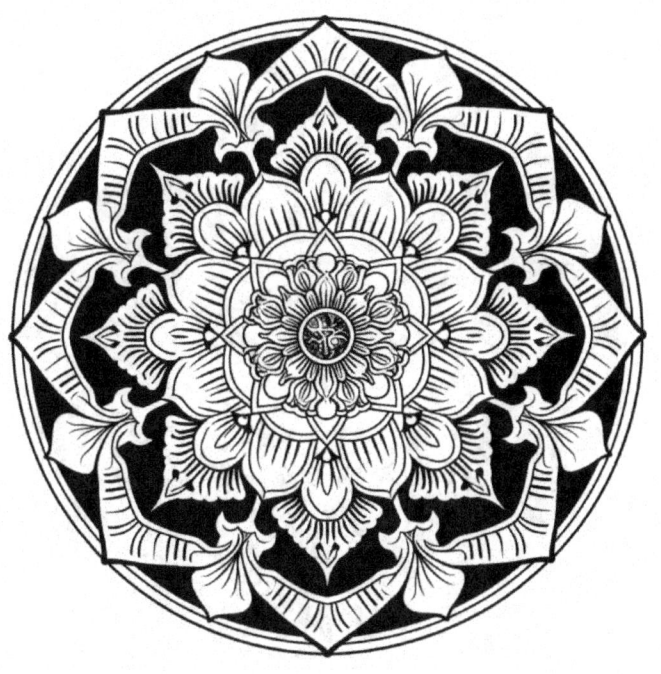

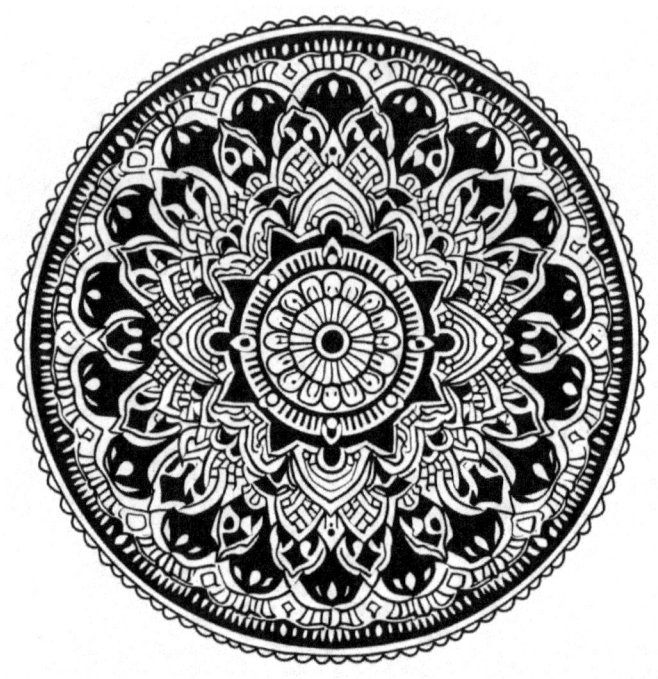

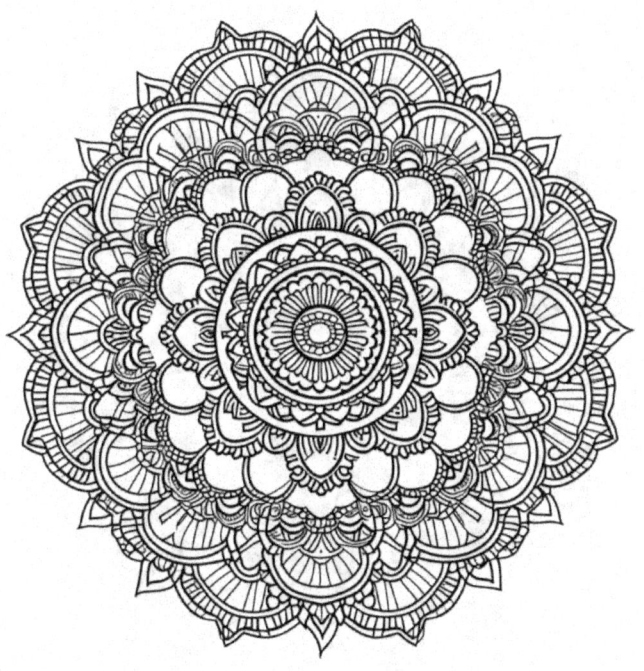

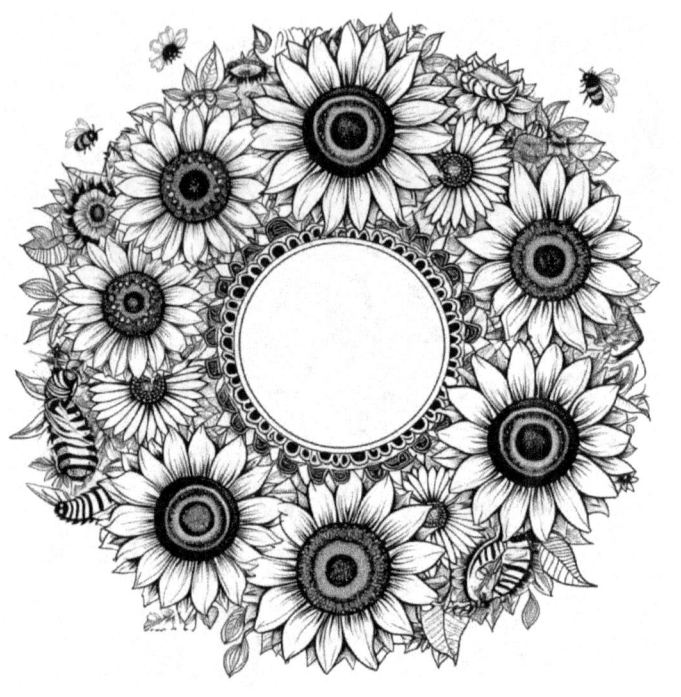

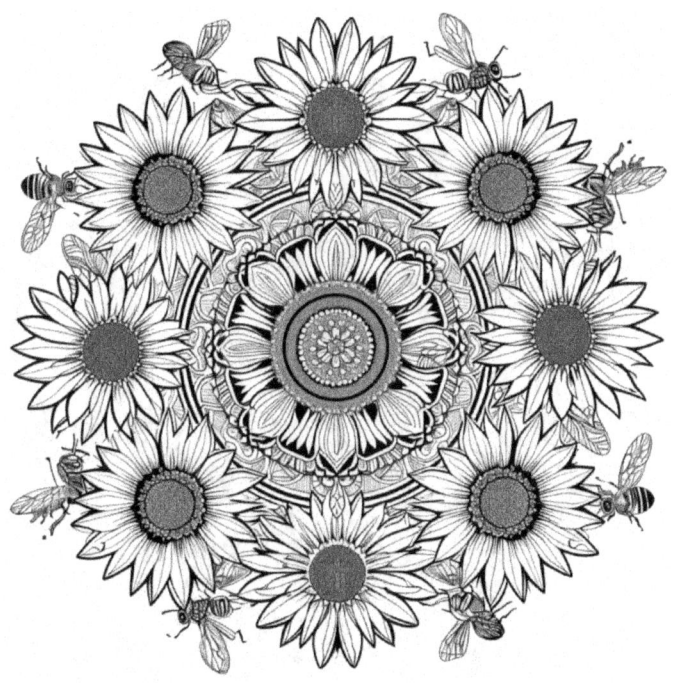

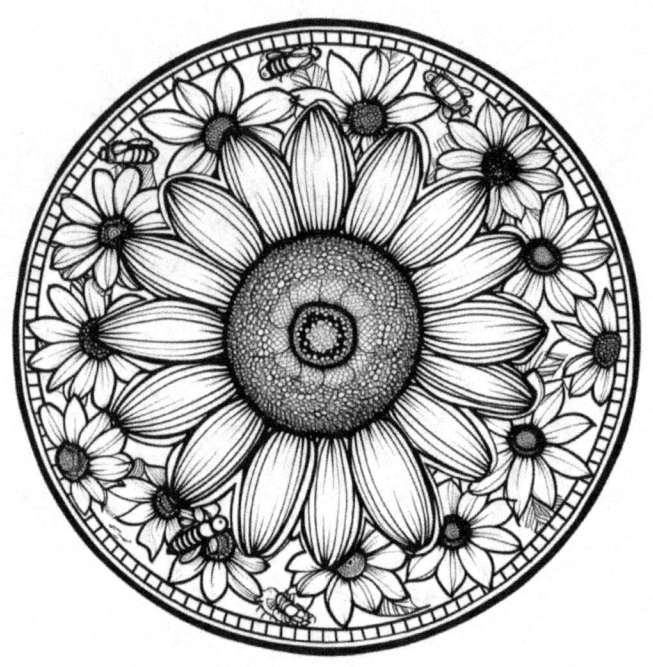

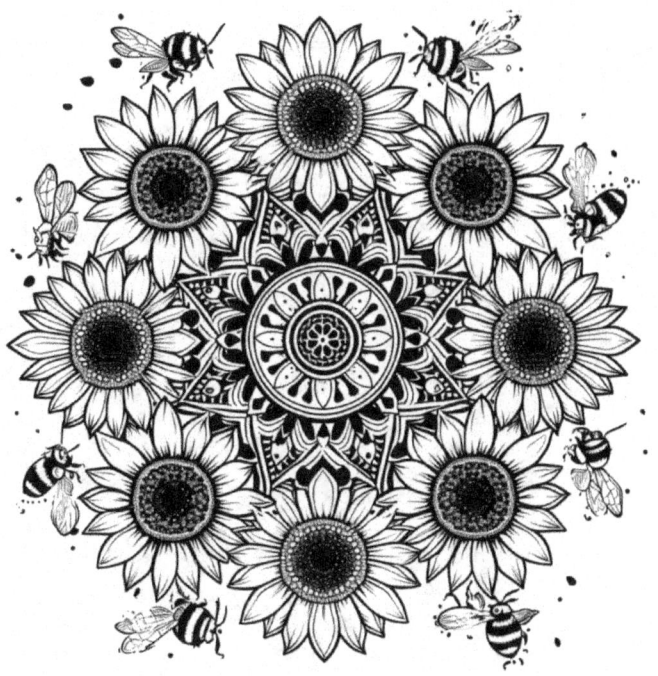

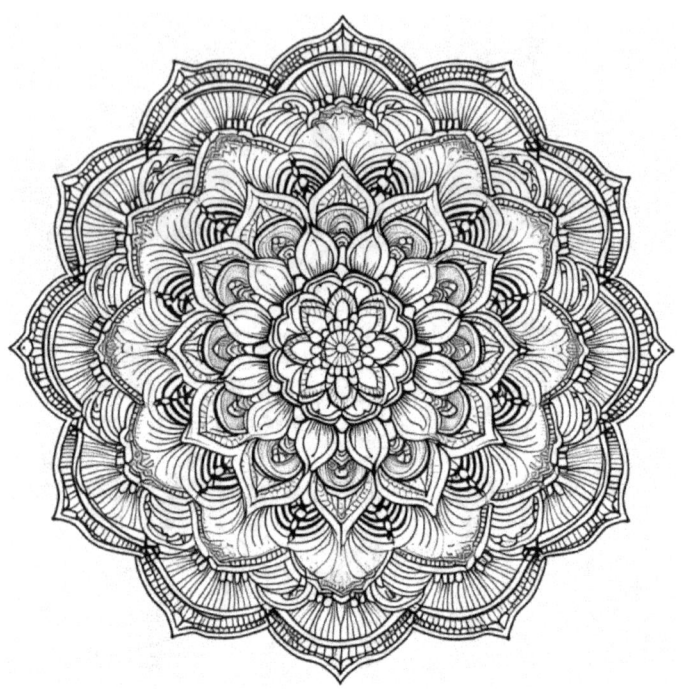

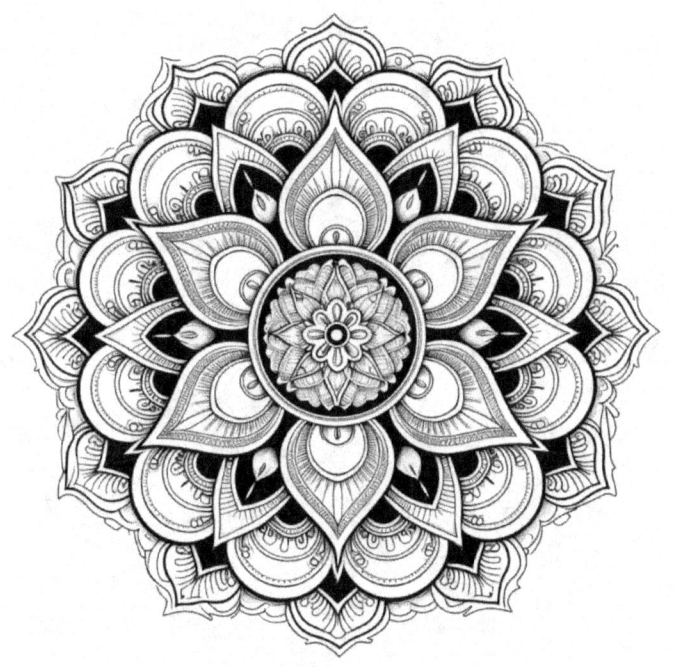

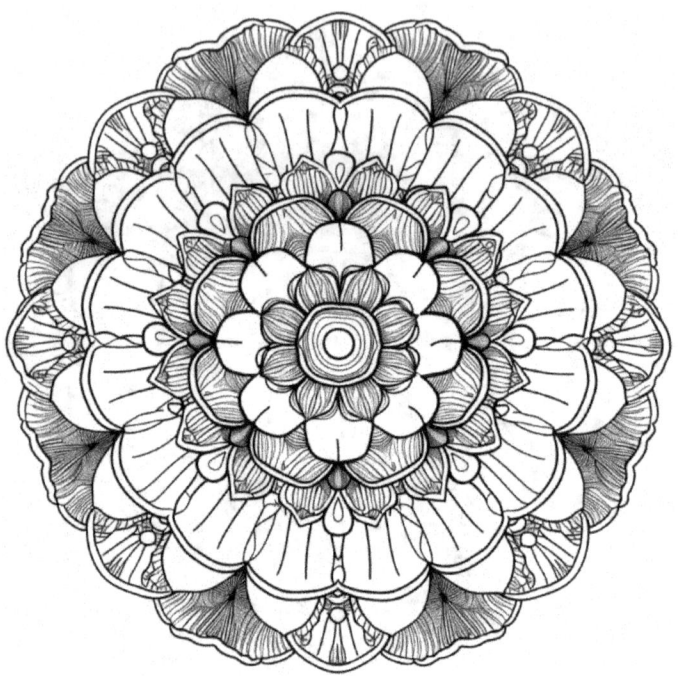

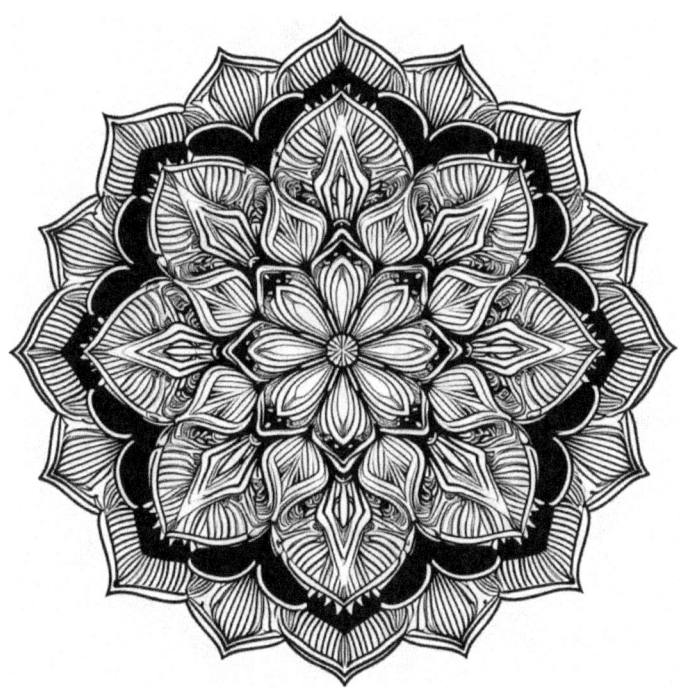

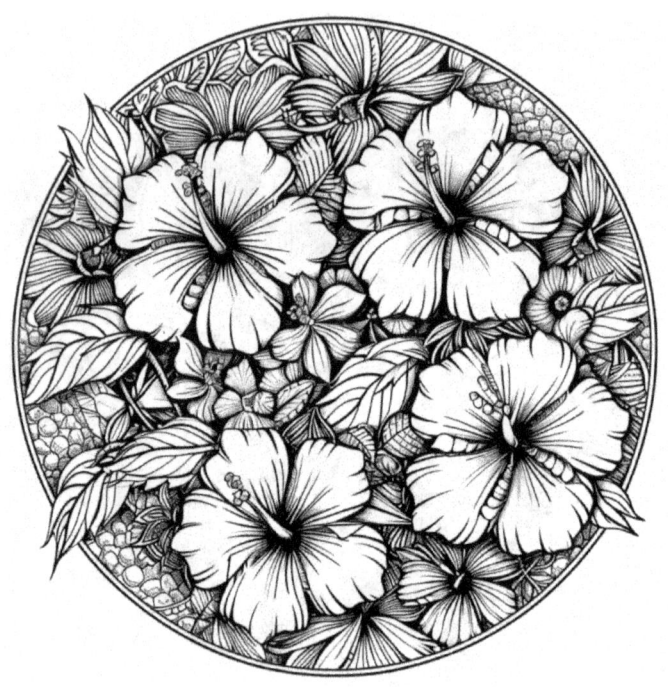

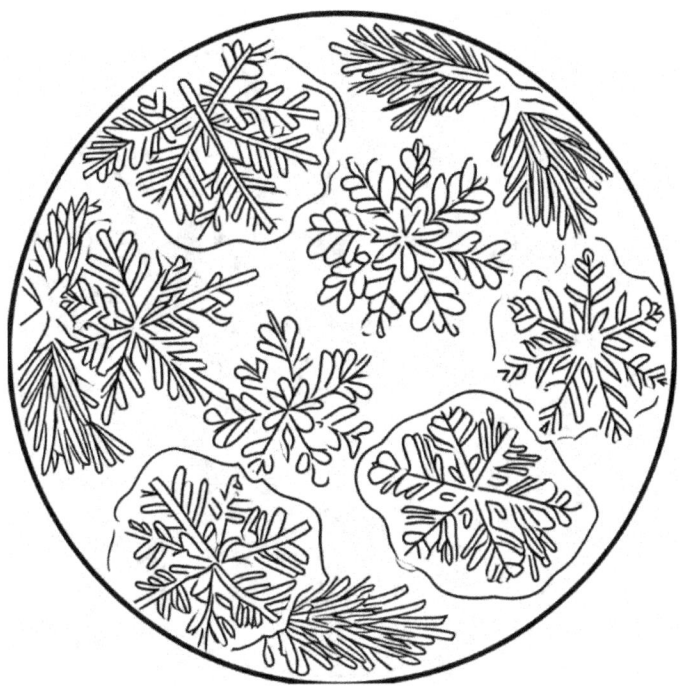

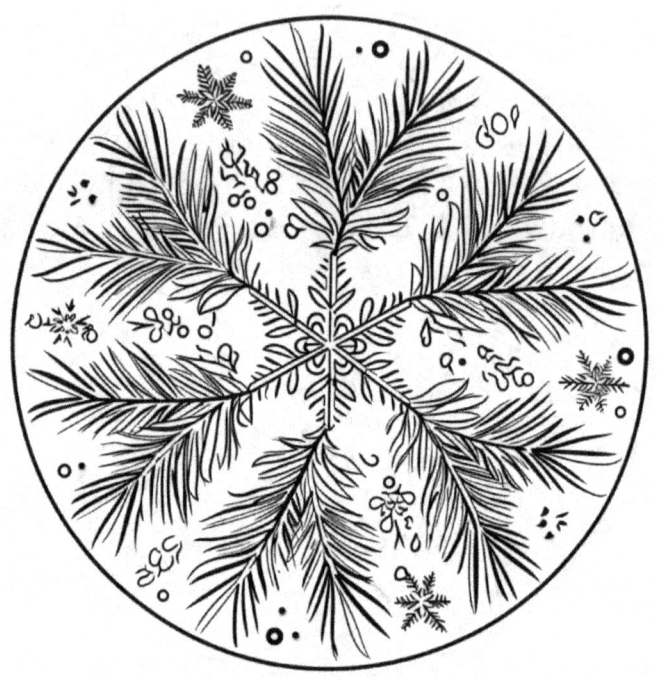

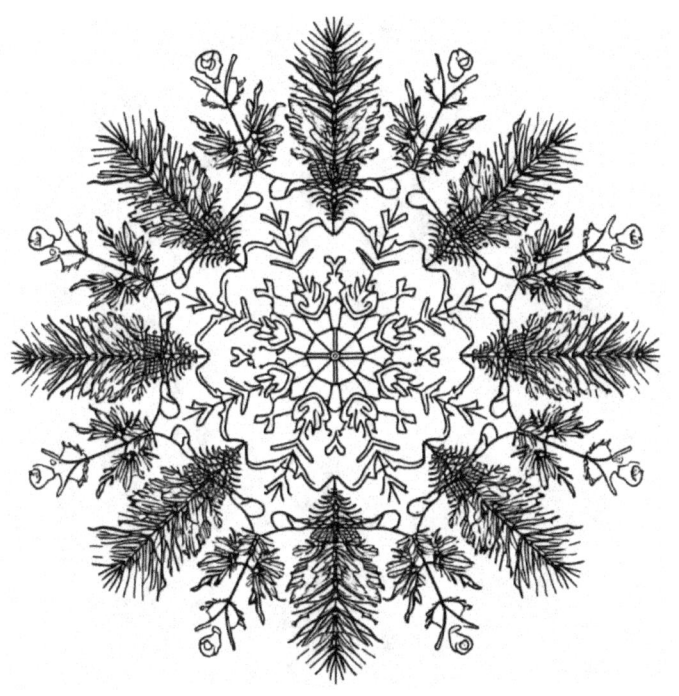

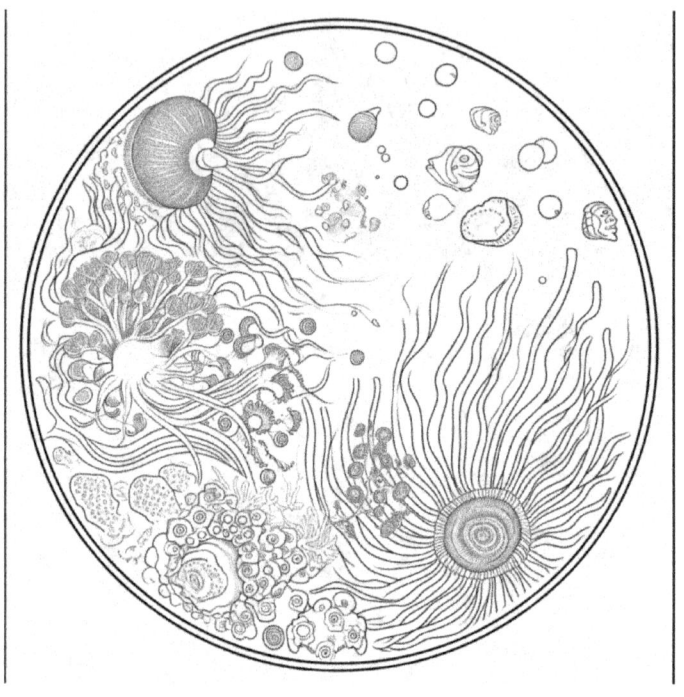

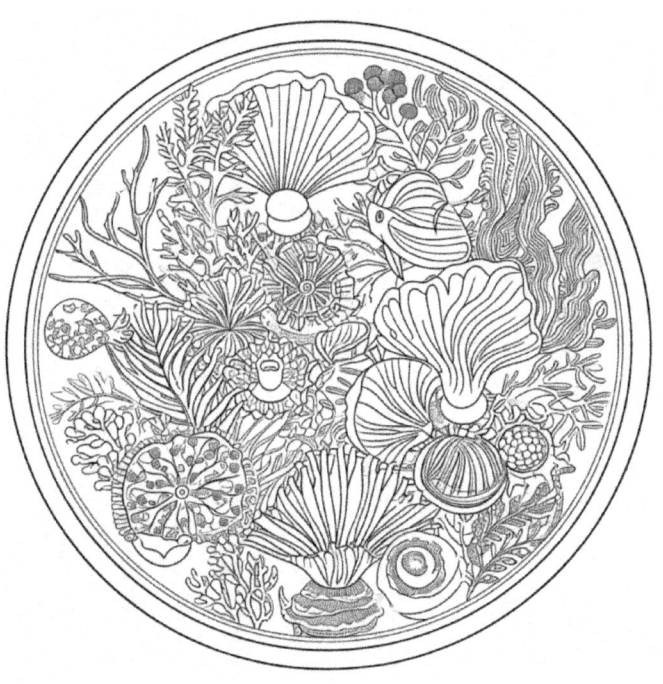

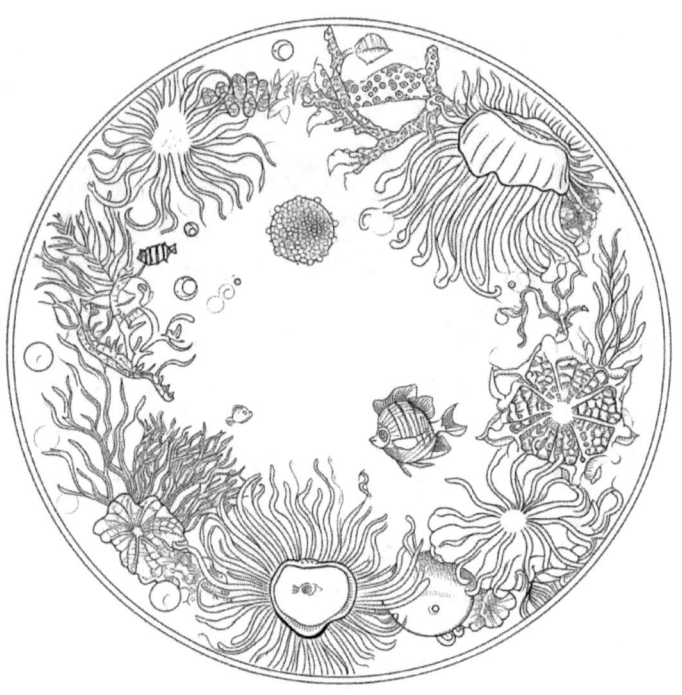

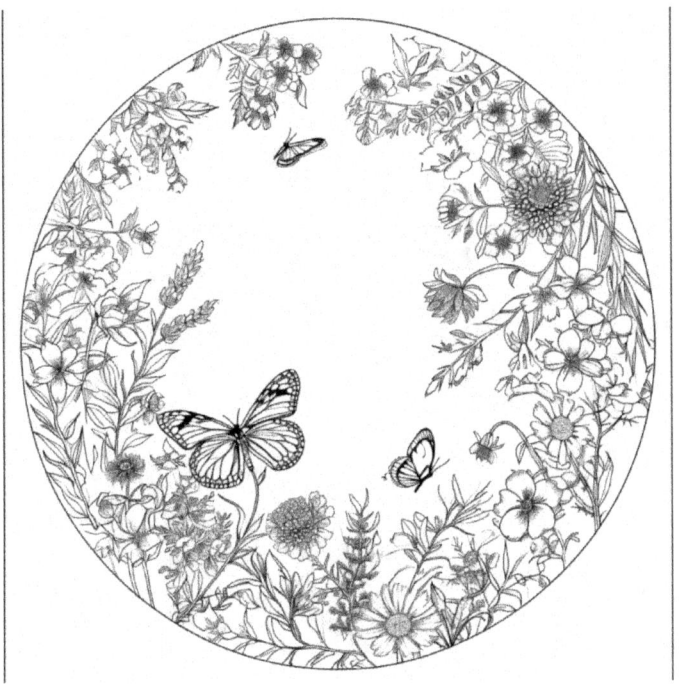

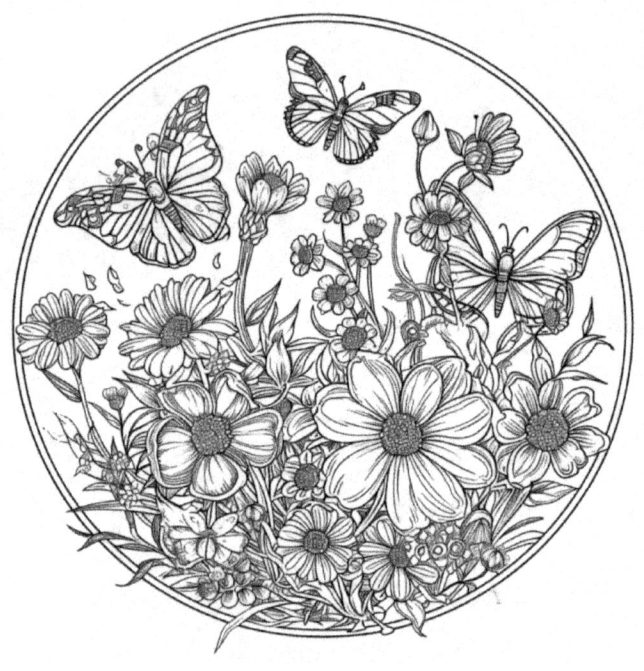

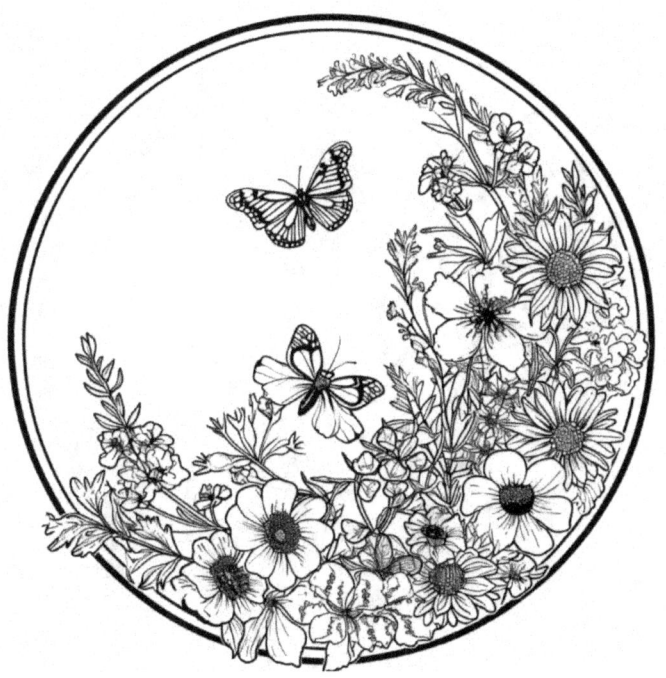

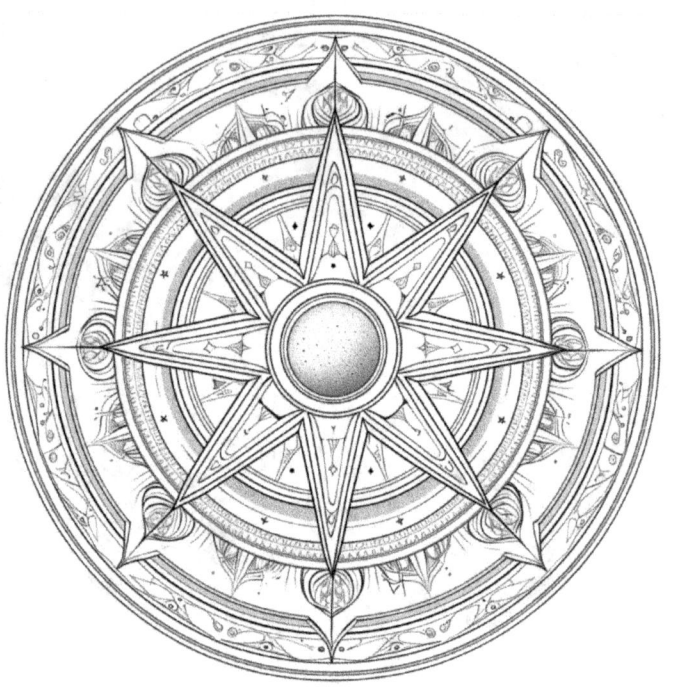

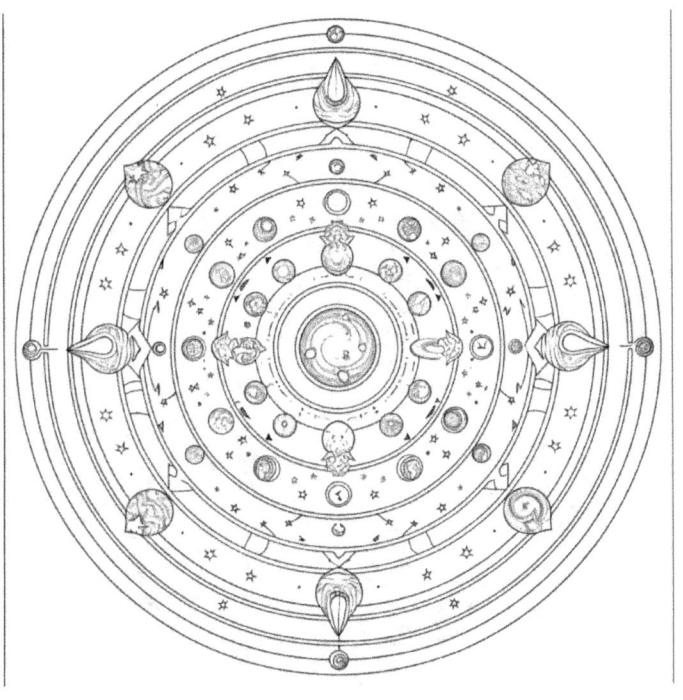

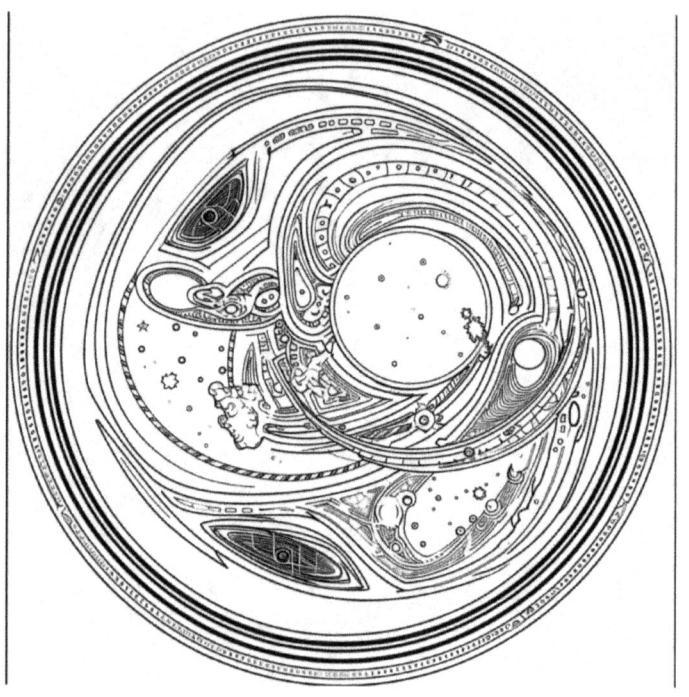

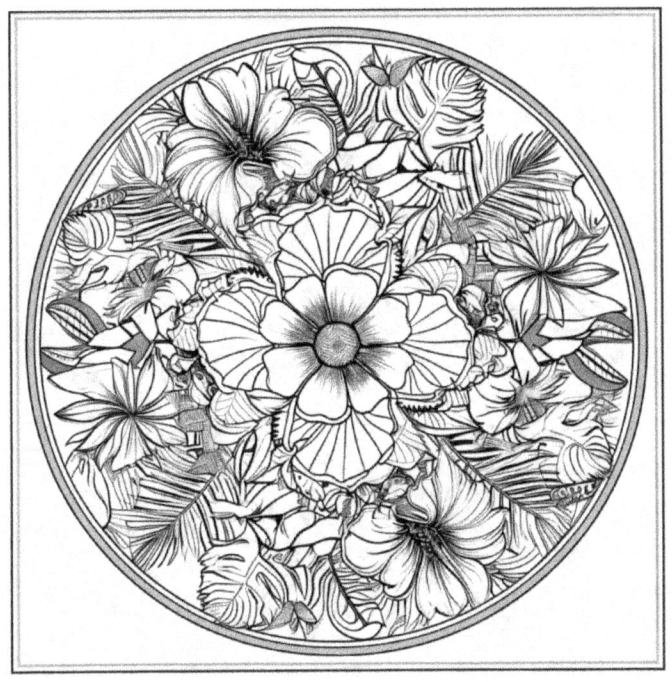

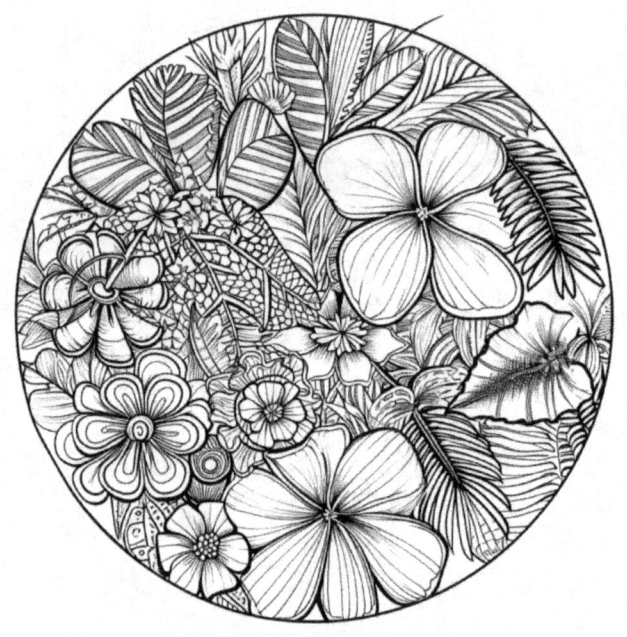

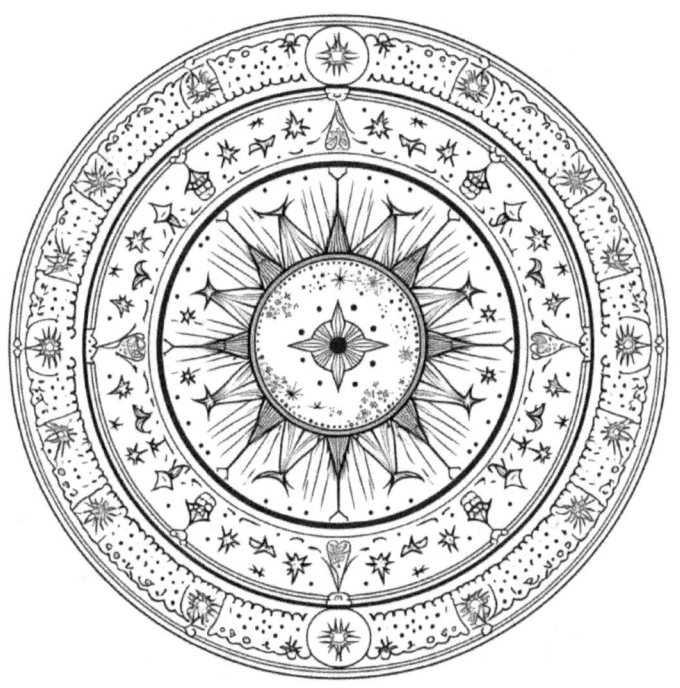

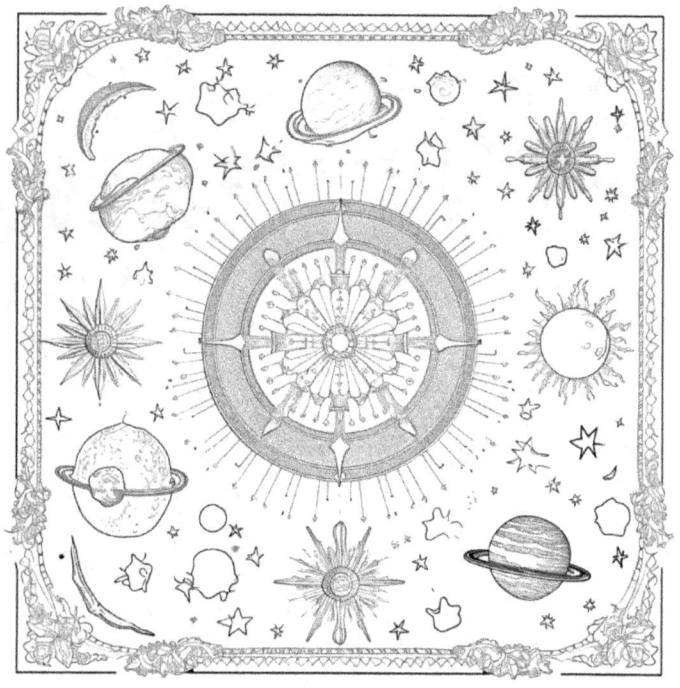

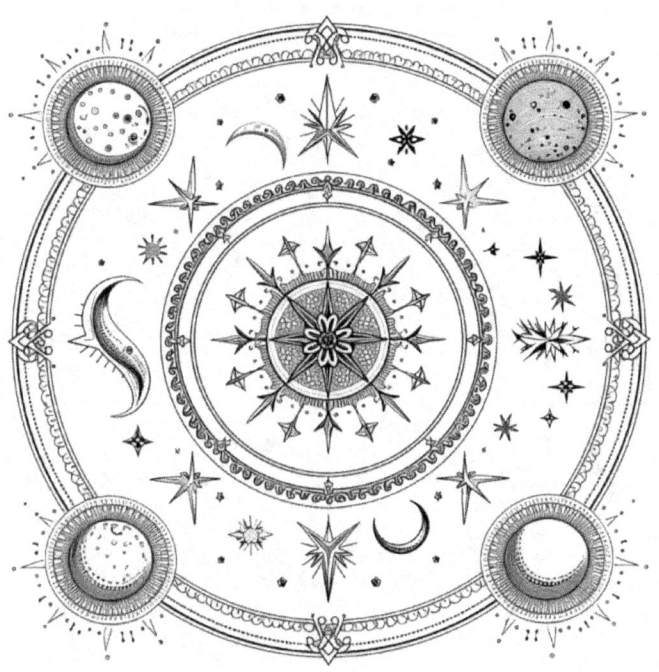

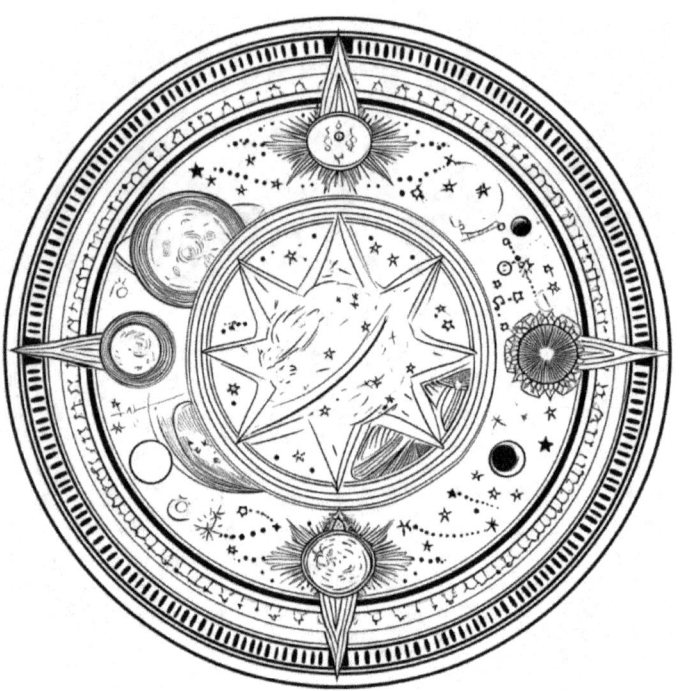

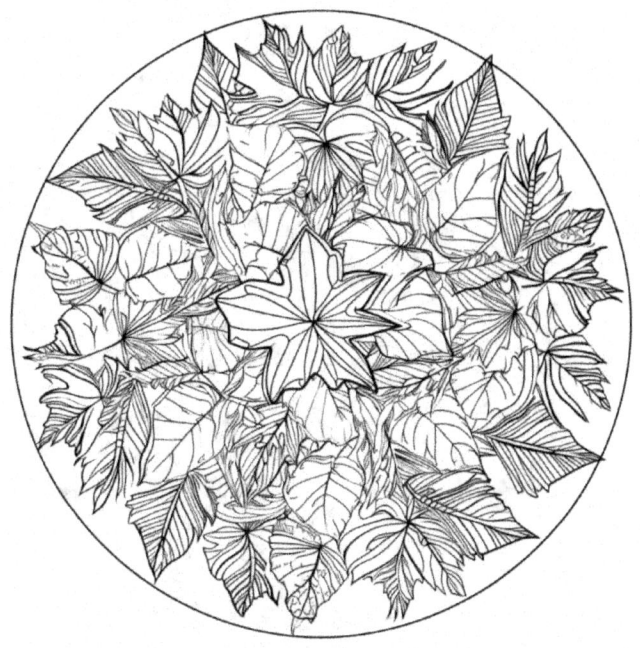

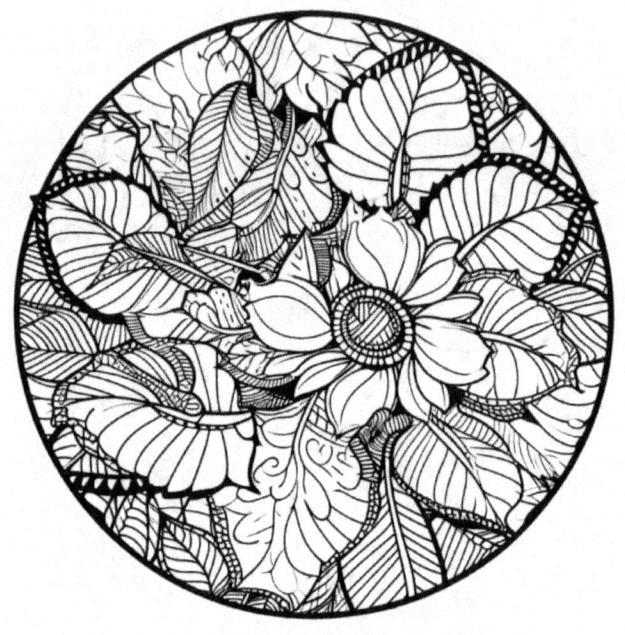

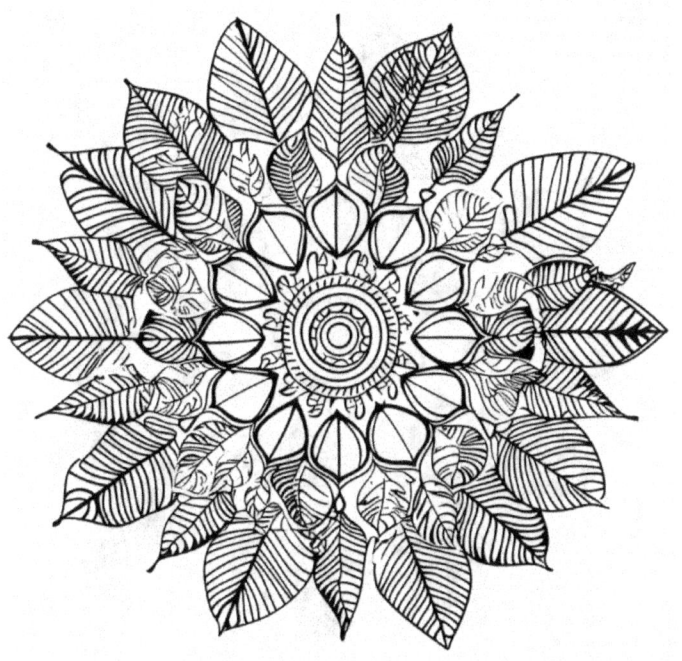

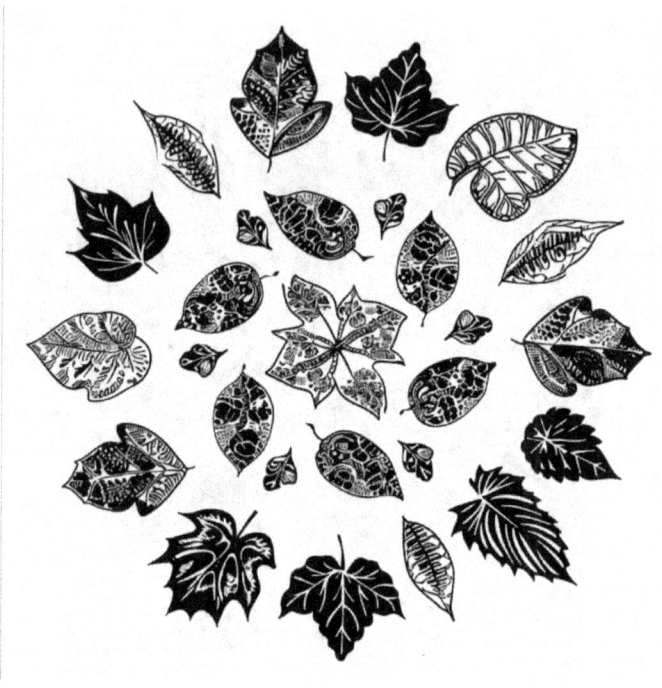

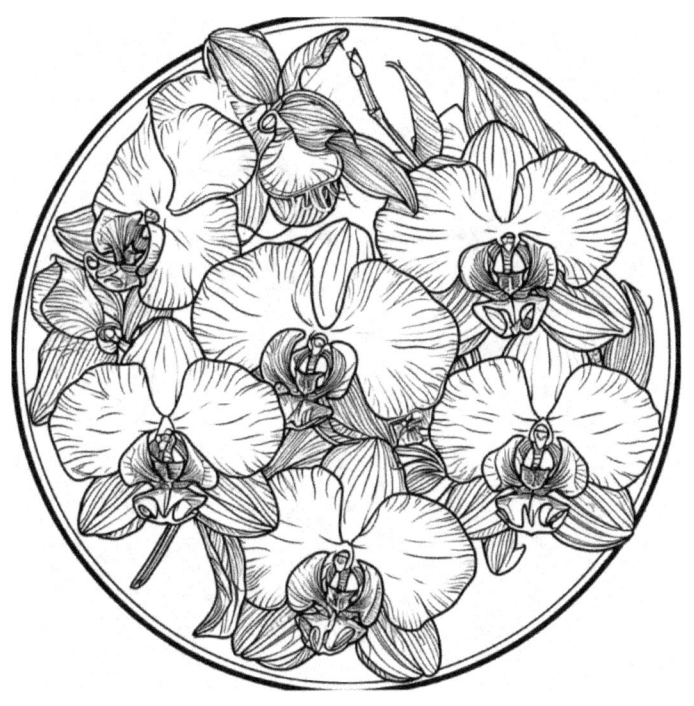

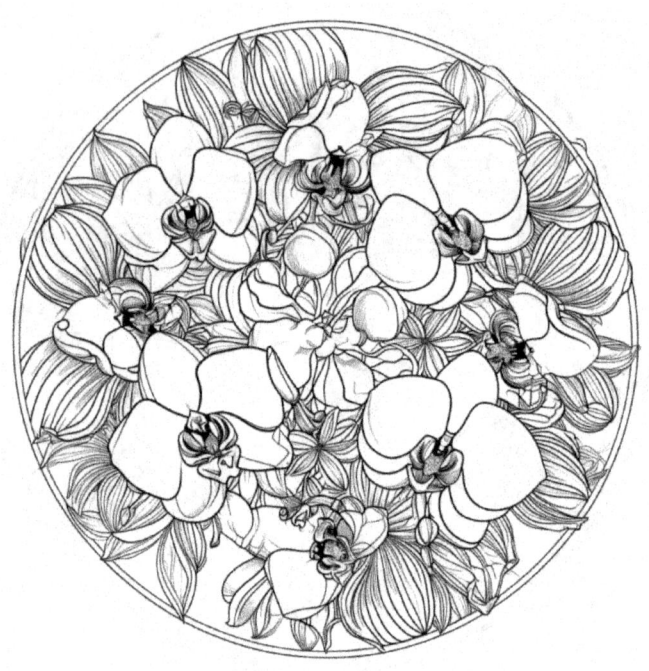

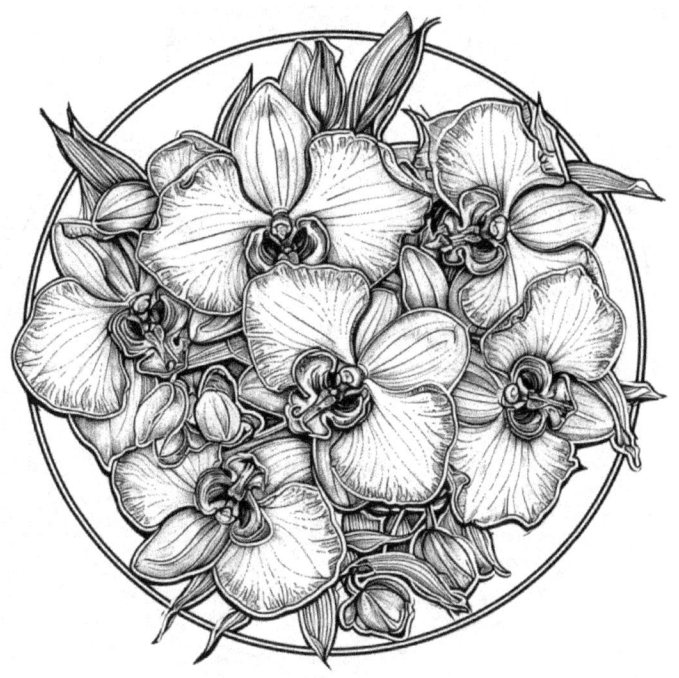

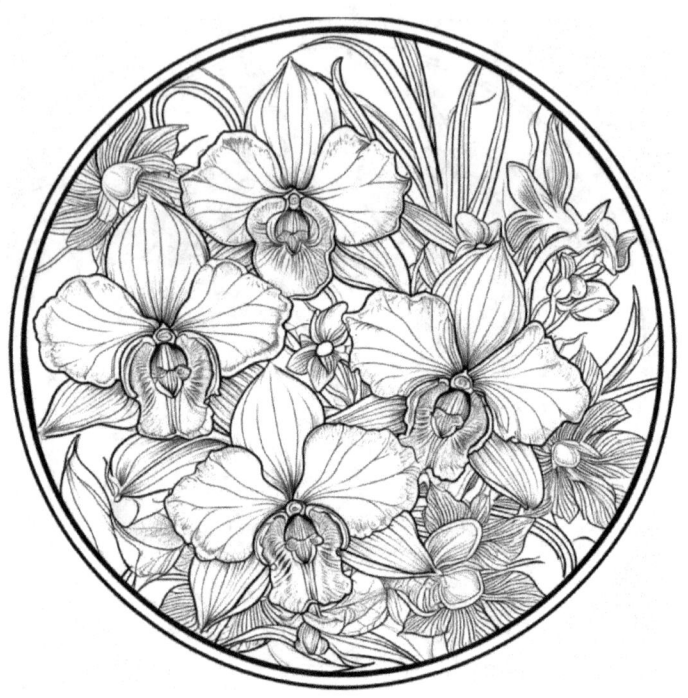

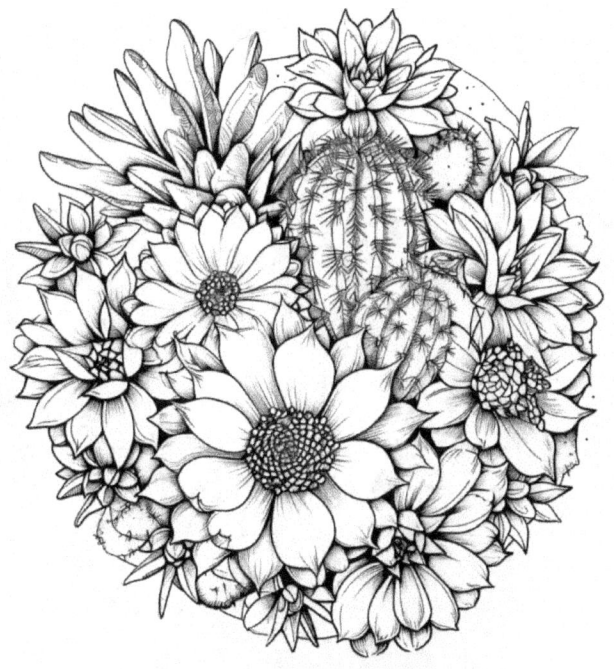

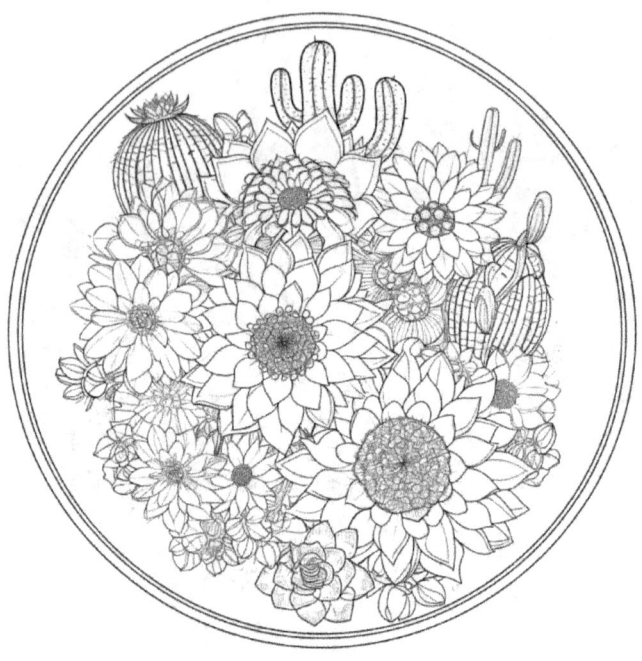

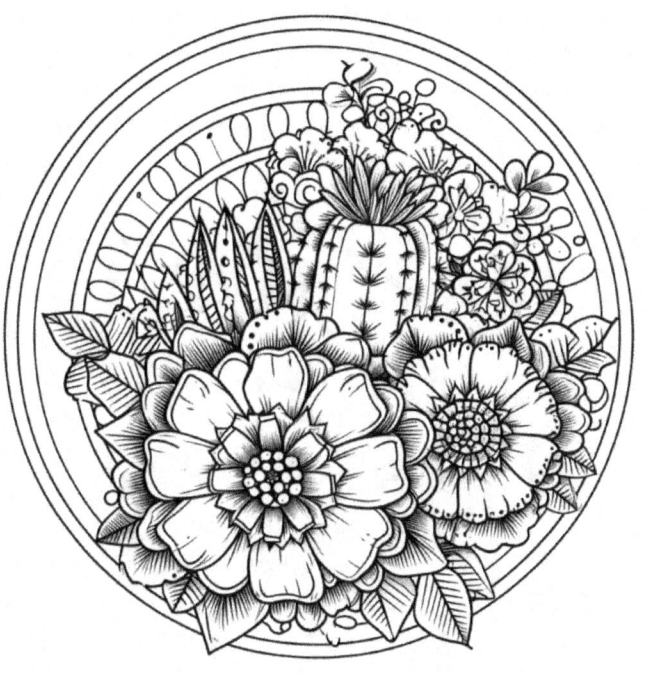

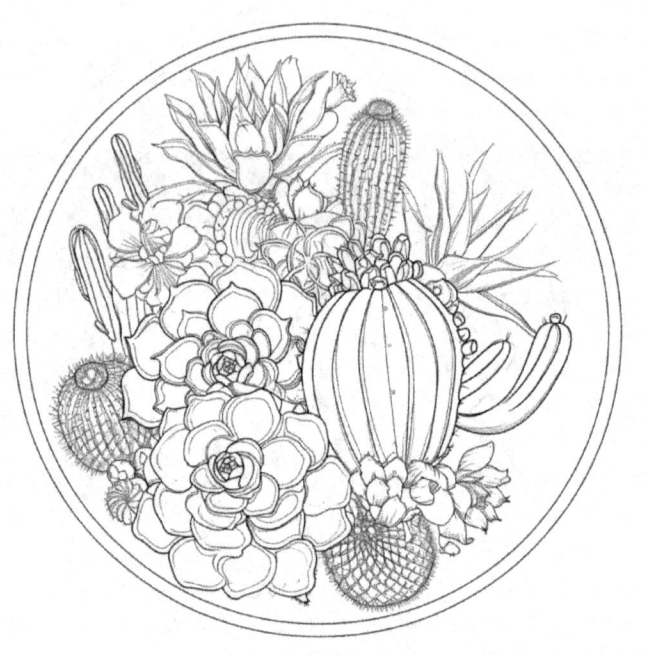

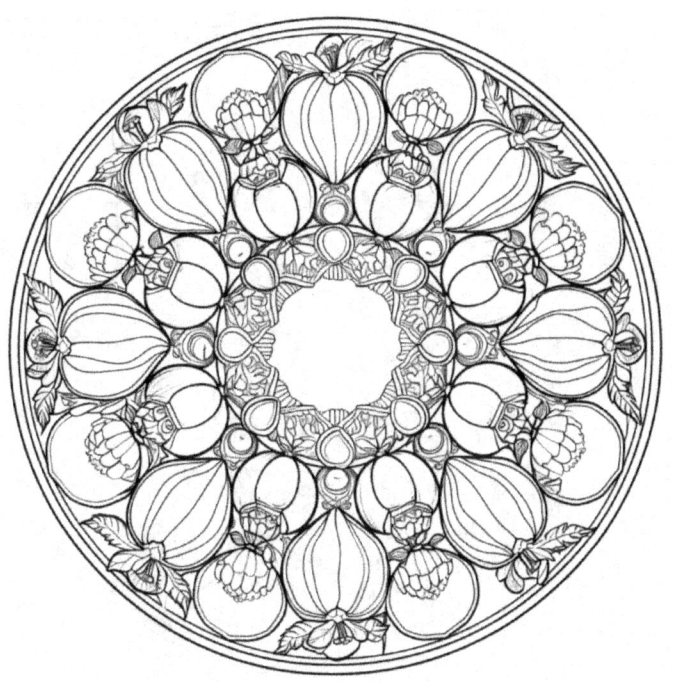

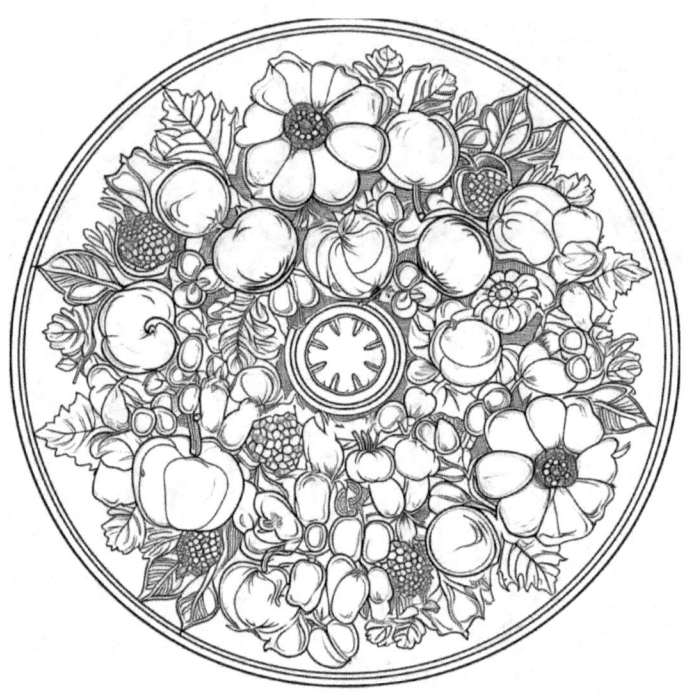

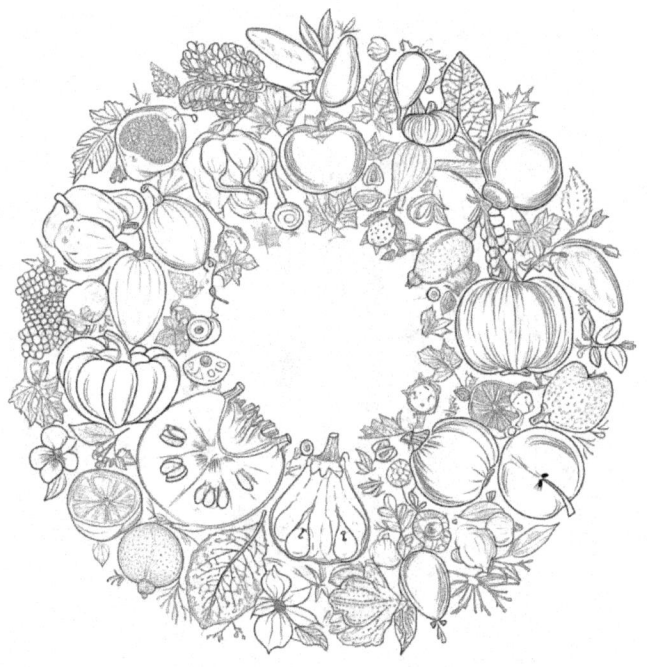

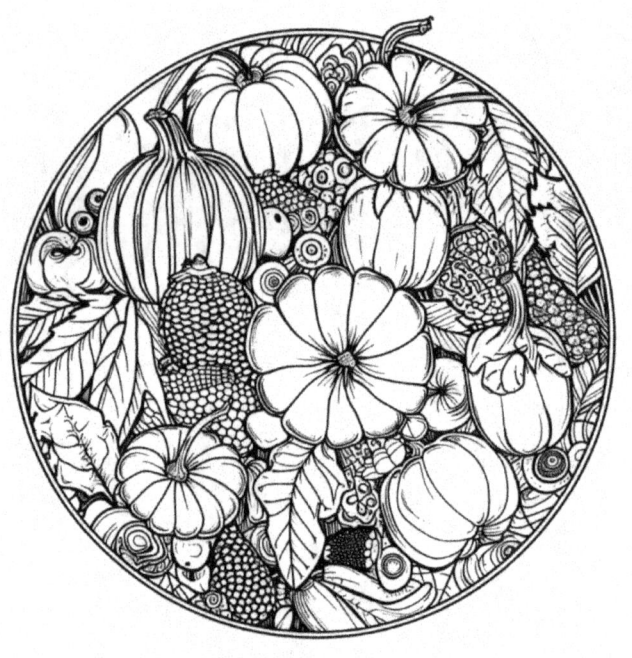

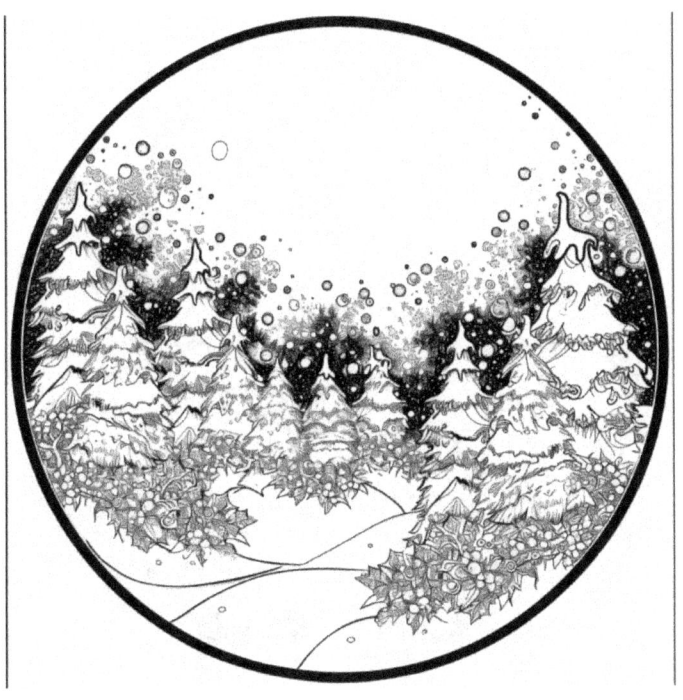

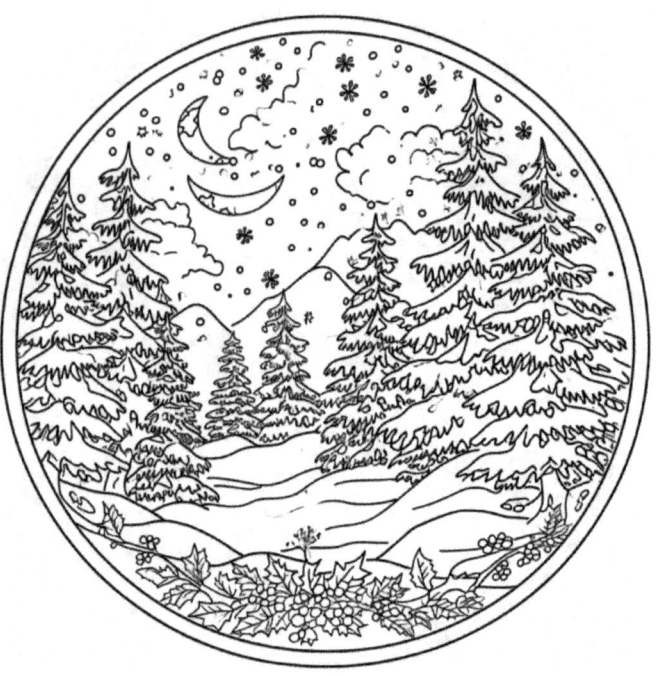

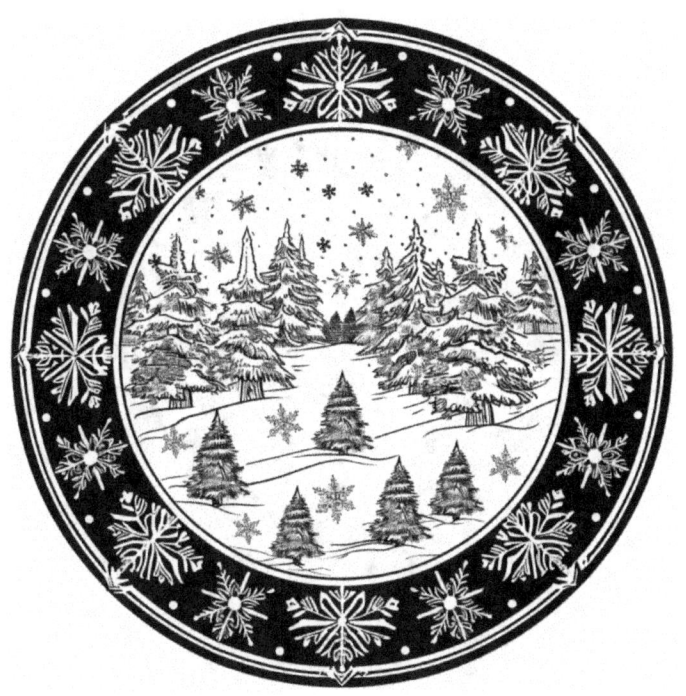

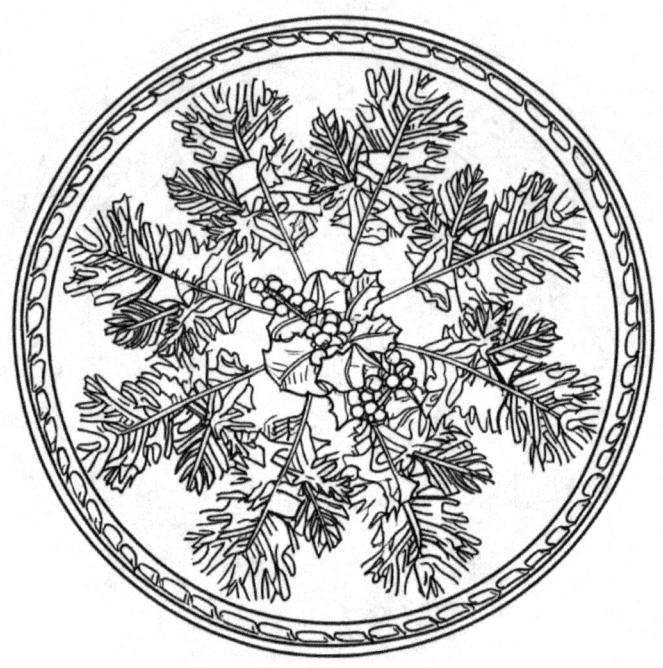

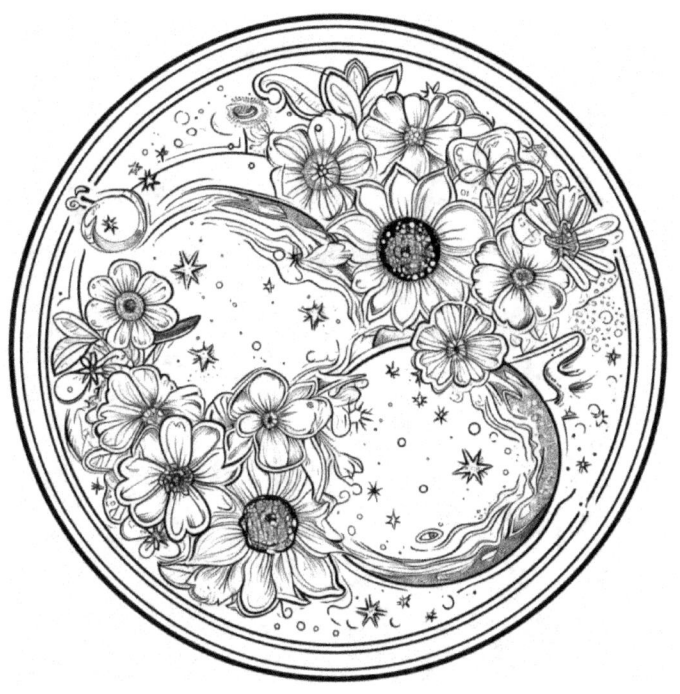

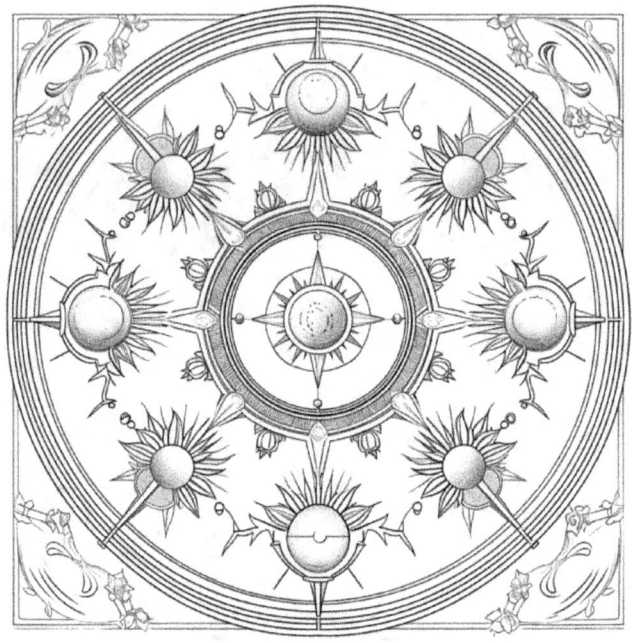

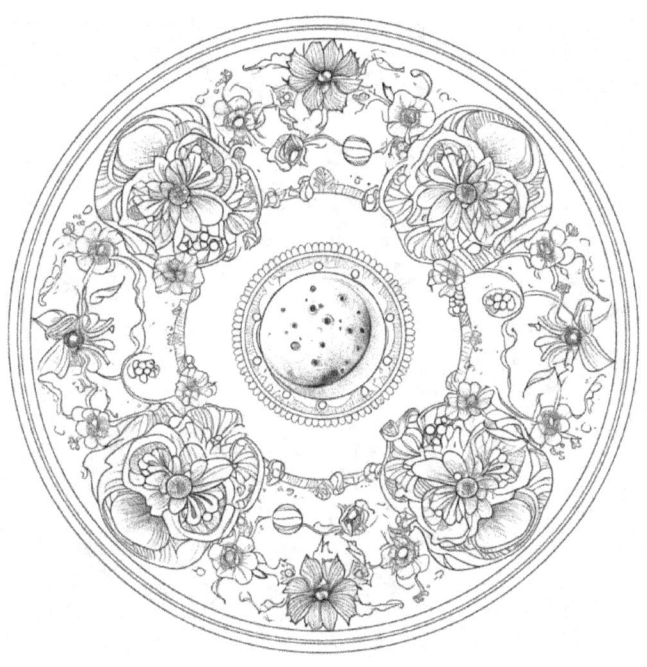

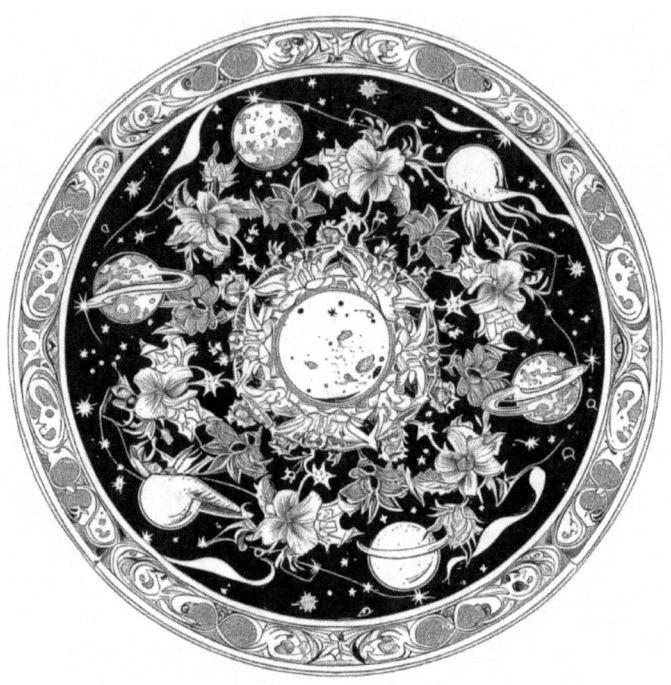

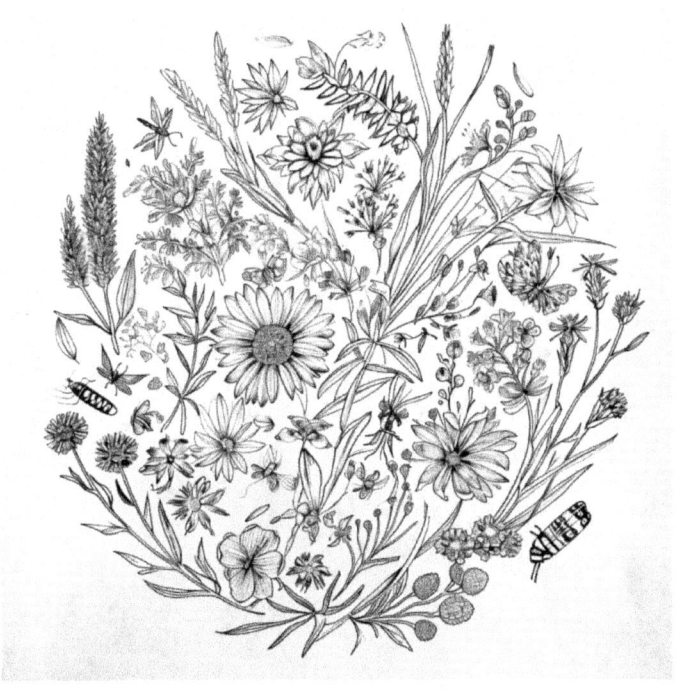

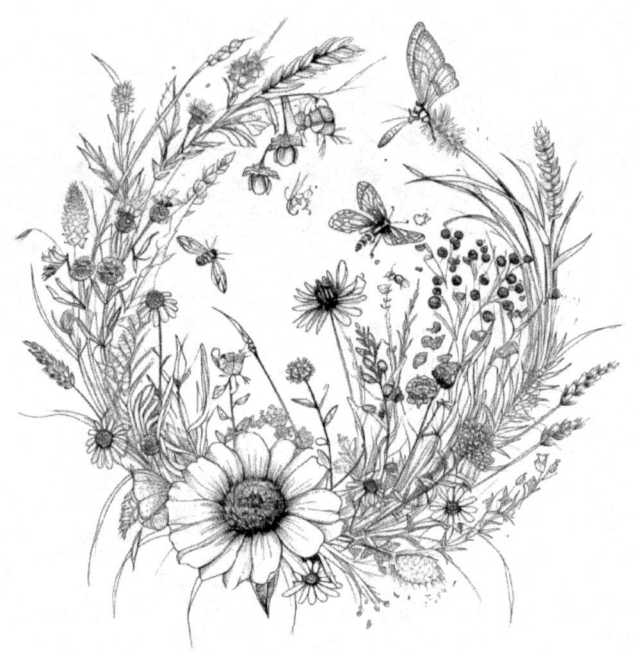

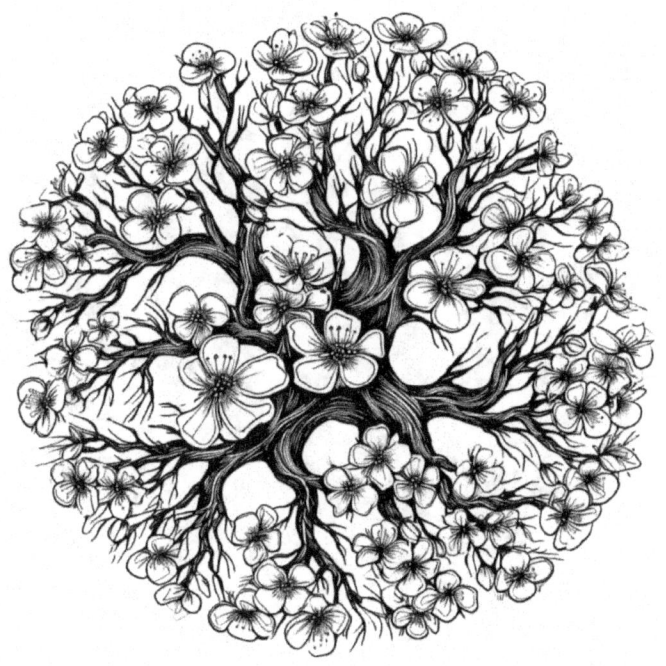

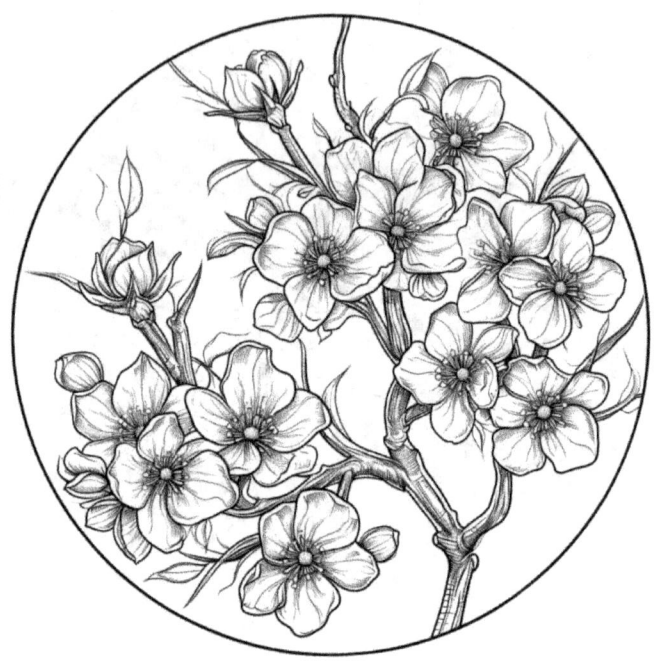

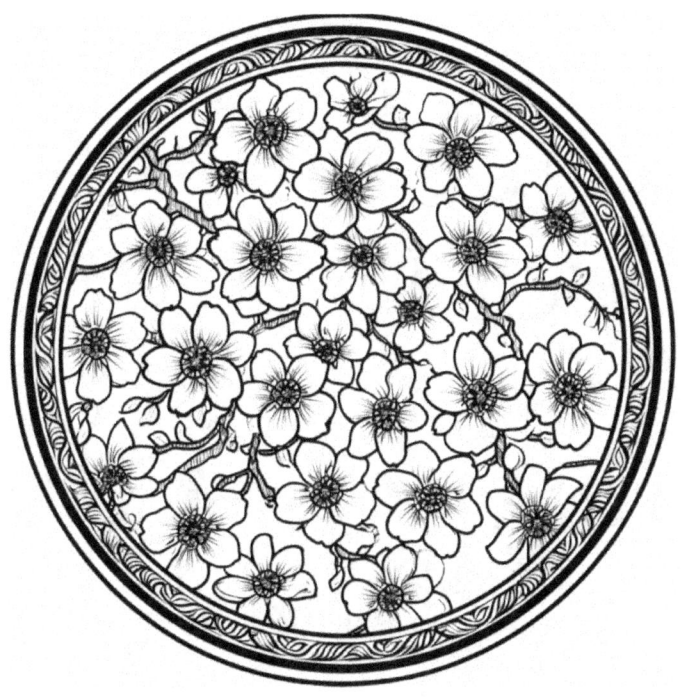

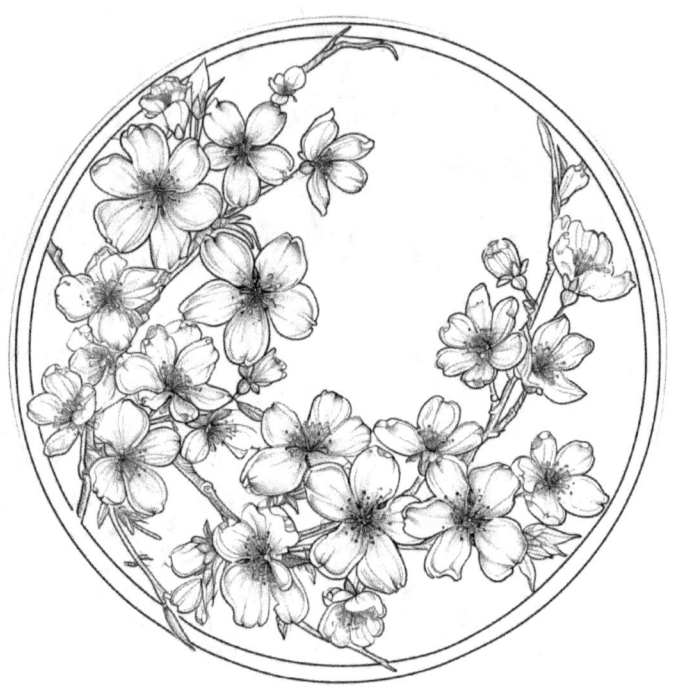

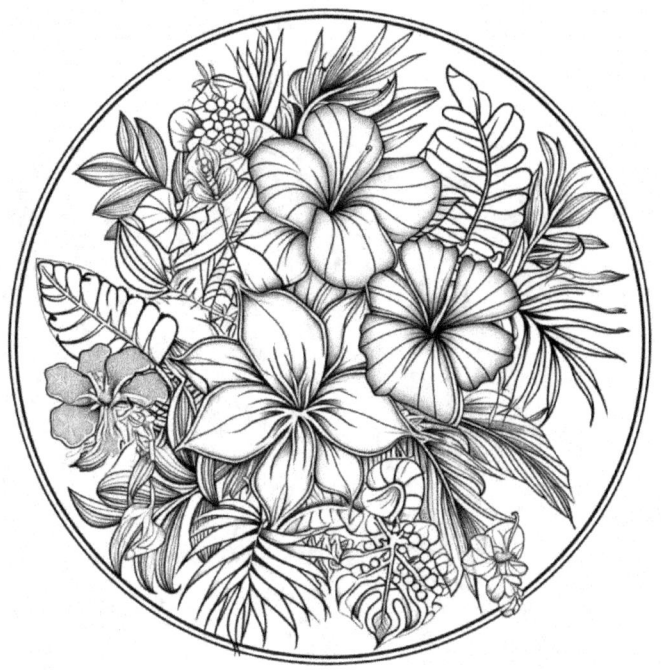

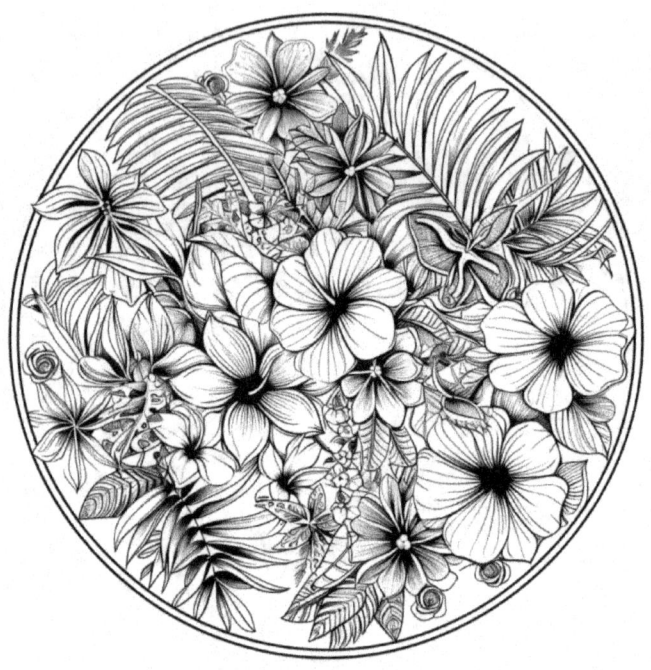

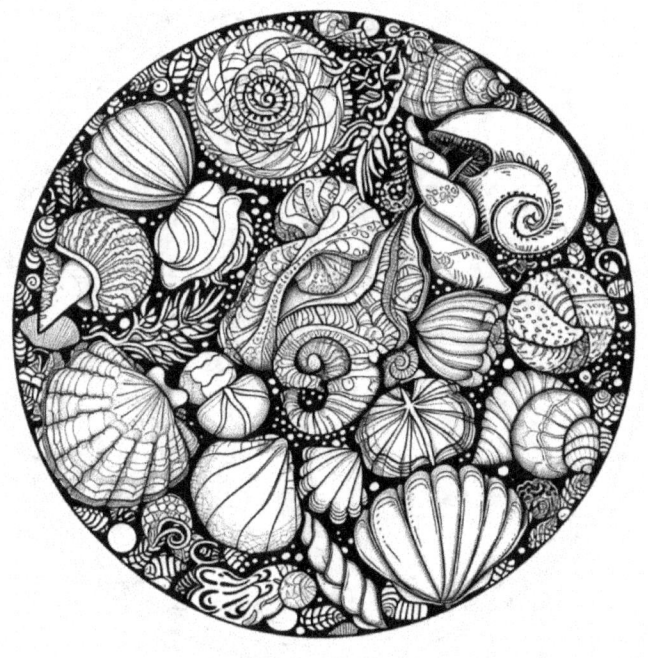

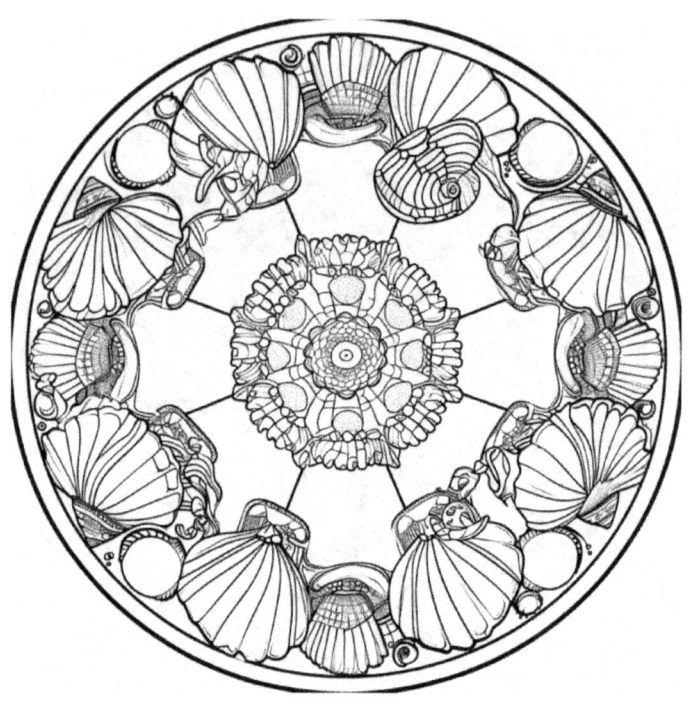

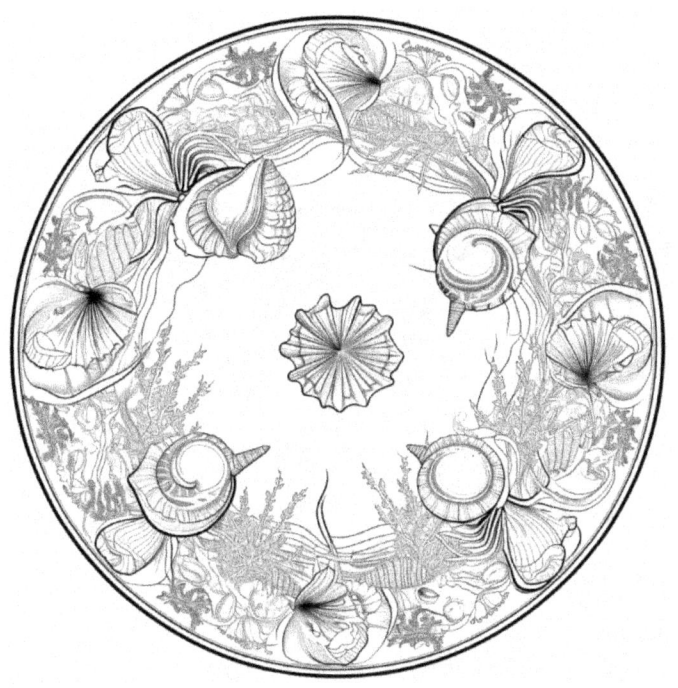

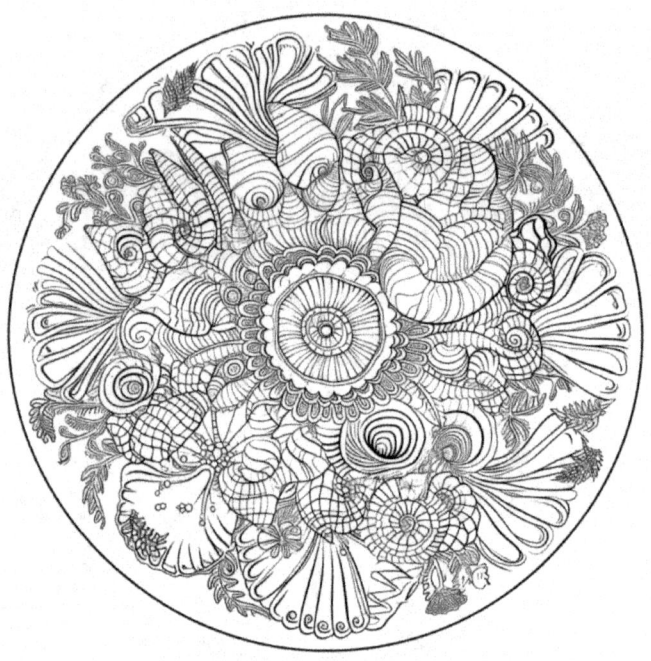

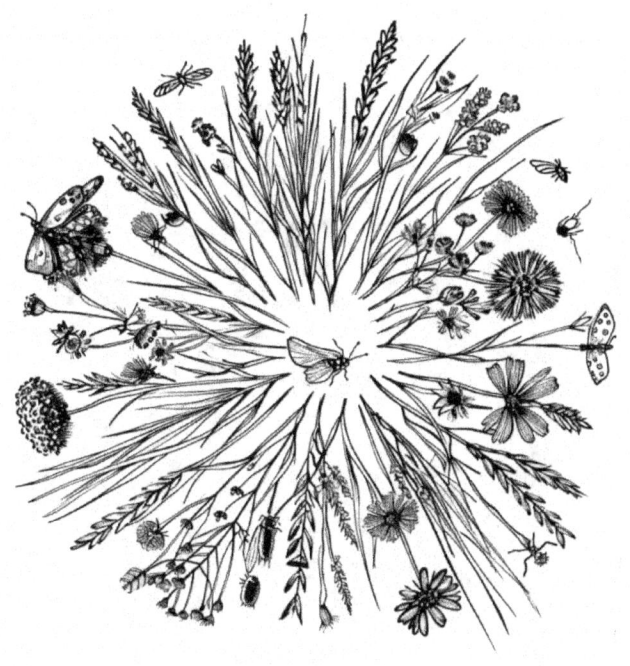

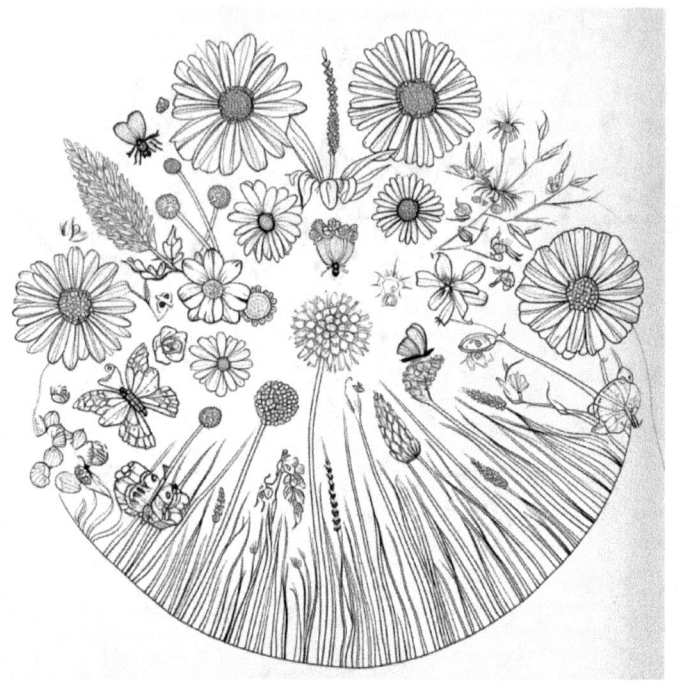

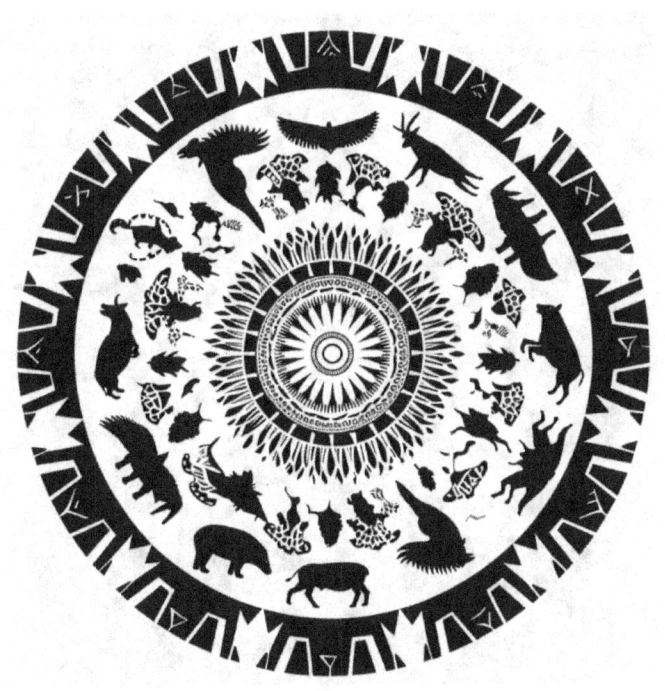

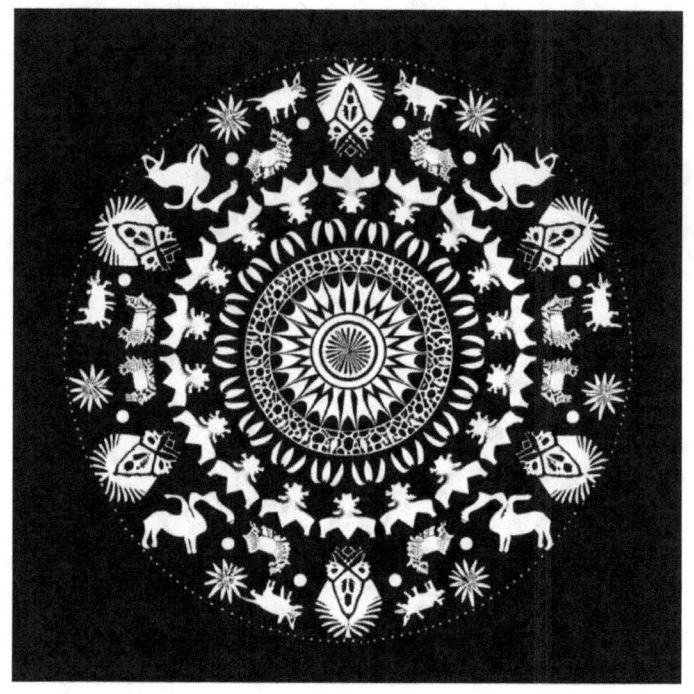

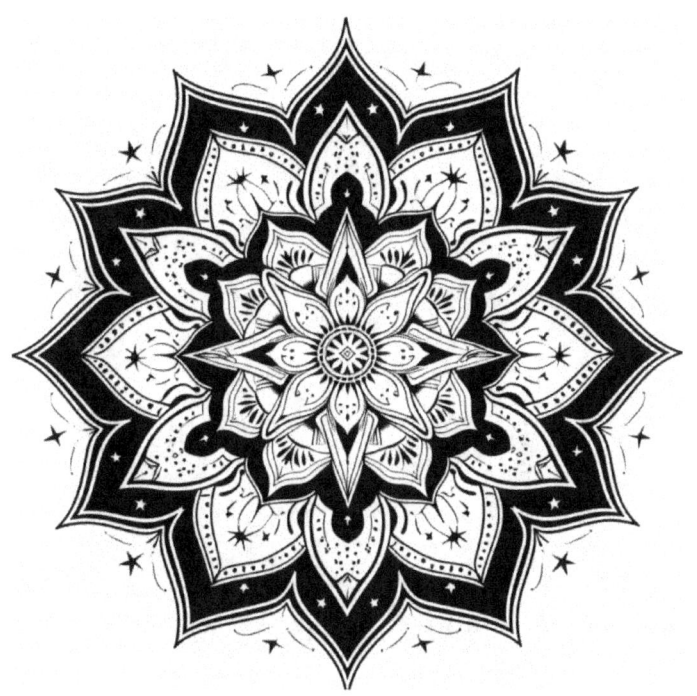

ABOUT THE AUTHOR

Lumina Visions is an artist who uses AI and new technologies to discover connections between art and Artificial Intelligence